JUDO

JUDO

Alex Butcher

THE LYONS PRESS

Guilford, Connecticut
An Imprint of the Globe Pequot Press

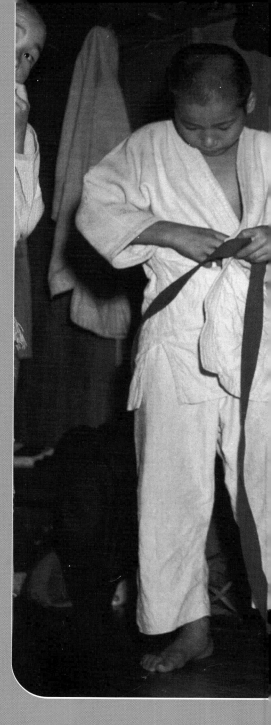

AUTHOR'S ACKNOWLEDGEMENTS

I would like to extend my sincere thanks to: my wife, Angela, for her years of under-standing and patience as a fellow *judoka*; Ian Geustyn, Commonwealth gold medallist, for all his help in making this book possible; Melanie and Eunice Geustyn, for making sure that this book became a reality; my daughter, Jessica, for her patience and help in simplifying the text; Madre Rinquest, one of our up-and-coming *judoka*, who shows such promise; Bruno Wertz, for taking punishment beyond the call of duty; Malcolm Collins and Ken Webber, as well as the members of the 3-Ks Judo Club; and the British Schools Judo Association, for inspiring this book. Thanks, too, to Umberto Masconi for his exemplary dedication, and to Simon Pooley and Kenny Rinquest for their help.

DEDICATION

For Alexander Percy Butcher (6th dan), father of Kodokan judo in South Africa:

'To ask is but a moment's shame, but not to ask and remain ignorant is a life-long shame.'

And for Patrick Stevenson, for being such a true inspiration and one of the finest *judoka* I have ever had the privi-lege of knowing.

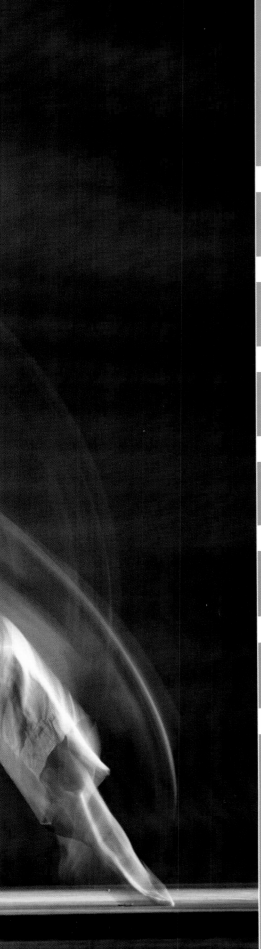

CONTENTS

INTRODUCTION

A brief history of judo

Judo, a martial art in which *judoka*, or judo players, use movement, balance and leverage to gain advantage over each other, is one of the fastest-growing sports in the world. Both men and women, young and old, practise this sport, which helps create good posture, balance, physical fitness and increased mental alertness.

Competitive judo

Competitive judo is widely practised throughout the world and many players practise and compete as a full-time occupation. Although the basic techniques are very simple and easy to learn, it takes many years of hard work and training to acquire the necessary experience to excel as a full-time professional.

Judo has been represented in the Olympics by men since the 1964 Games in Tokyo and by women since the 1992 Games in Barcelona. It is thus an ever-growing sport that is constantly being enhanced and adapted by *judoka* at international level.

Using this book

This book is primarily a visual introduction to judo, but the images presented here do not constitute a comprehensive manual and are intended to illustrate the most common and popular techniques in competitive judo. Many have been specifically selected for this book, and variations on the techniques may well exist.

Wherever possible, the English equivalent of Japanese terms for specific techniques have been provided to make the book more accessible. Other basic terms are fully explained and the words accurately translated according to the official *Kodokan New Japanese–English Dictionary of Judo*, published by the Kodokan Judo Institute in August 2000.

Because judo improves minor and major coordination skills and low muscle tone, it is practised in many countries as a school sport. Judo teaches self-discipline and encourages children to deal with physical aggression in a constructive manner. In certain countries, the existence of national school judo associations helps to develop judo to its fullest potential. The collaboration between the British Schools Judo Association and the British Judo Association is an excellent example of the beneficial relationship that can exist between a school and a national sporting body. This has produced a number of the UK's most successful competitors and Olympic medallists. Many started judo at school and, with help, guidance and encouragement, they were able to reach their full potential.

As a martial art, judo utilizes throwing techniques, grappling techniques and arm locks. When combined, these are a very effective form of self-defence. *Judoka* also use various strangulation techniques that attempt to cut off the blood or air supply or both, and defeat an opponent while being held down. *Judoka* learn, too, how to defend themselves against the strangulation techniques that are applied by skilled judo opponents. As a consequence of this particular type of training, judo players are especially adept at self-defence.

Judo has also recently been adapted so that it can be practised by physically disabled individuals such as the visually impaired and is now acknowledged as a Paralympic sport.

When a *judoka* retires from the competitive arena, it does not signify the end of the player's participation in the sport, as one can then concentrate on judo as an art that can be practised until an advanced age.

opposite A POPULAR CREDO AMONG *JUDOKA* IS 'IN SPIRIT UNITED, IN SKILL OPPOSED'.

In the beginning

Jigoro Kano, born on 28 October 1860, founded the martial art form known as Kodokan judo in 1882 by reformulating and adapting classical jujutsu systems. The popular form of judo that is presently practised around the world is a further adaptation that signifies a growing and expanding sport.

As a young man, Jigoro Kano was not physically strong. At the age of 18, in order to overcome his weak constitution, he began to study jujutsu, a system of combat against armed or unarmed opponents using either short-weapon techniques such as stabbing and slashing, or empty-handed techniques such as hitting, kicking or choking. He practised jujutsu largely with two schools and encountered different approaches to technique. The Tenshin Shinyo-ryu (system, style or school) stressed striking, joint locks and strangulation and the Kito-ryu emphasized lower-body skills and throwing. Jigoro Kano decided to concentrate on the best techniques from each and sought to identify the underlying principle that linked the various methods of jujutsu.

Jigoro Kano graduated from Tokyo University in 1881, and Kodokan Judo was officially founded in 1882. Jigoro Kano spent many hours formulating a new system of defence by eliminating dangerous jujutsu actions, retaining certain techniques and adding a philosophy of mental and physical training. The *ju* in judo is derived from the Chinese, meaning 'gentle' or 'soft', while the *do* means 'way' — thus the term *ju-do* means 'gentle way'. Although judo was founded in 19th-century Japan, the term *ju-do* predates the sport by almost two millennia and linguistic historians have traced the term to the chronicles of the first-century Chinese Emperor Kuang Wu. As a dominant language of East Asia, Chinese greatly influenced the writing systems and vocabularies of neighbouring countries such as Japan. Thus, although native Japanese constitutes the largest portion of the language, Japanese still includes words borrowed in earlier history from Chinese.

The way, or *do*, of judo was of great importance to Jigoro Kano and he thus named it Kodokan judo — the *ko* meaning lecture or practice, the *do* meaning way and the *kan* a hall or place in which to practise. The Kodokan emblem visually emphasizes the core judo principle that 'the soft can control the hard' with the representation of a piece of red-hot iron surrounded by white silk. The white signifies a soft outside and the red a hard inner.

JUDO REMAINS A POPULAR COMBAT SPORT FOR JAPANESE CHILDREN, BUT IS NOW ALSO WIDELY PRACTISED THORUGHOUT THE WORLD.

JAPAN IS HAILED AS THE BIRTHPLACE OF KODOKAN JUDO, AND IT WAS HERE THAT THE FIRST *DOJO* WAS ESTABLISHED IN 1882.

The origins of judo

The first *dojo* was in the grounds of the Eisho-ji Temple in Tokyo and comprised just nine members in 1882. The first students did not pay fees and were provided with every facility possible. To fund the *dojo*, Jigoro Kano worked late into the night translating texts, but great interest was generated in 1886 when the Tokyo Metropolitan Police Board held a tournament between the Kodokan and the Totsuka — one of the biggest jujutsu schools. Kano's *judoka* won with 13 bouts and drew the remaining two.

In 1888, the Kodokan finally won its contest with the jujutsu schools. The contest over which system of self-defence was to be used by the Japanese police had lasted two years, and the throwing techniques of two of Kano's original pupils, Saigo Shiro and Yokoyama Sakujiro, played an important part in this victory.

Eventually, judo superseded jujutsu in popularity, not only among the Japanese police but the country as a whole. Contests were originally an open event where competitors of all weights fought together, but weight groups were finally differentiated at the 16th Olympiad in Tokyo in 1964, with three weight classes — light-weight, middleweight and heavyweight — and an open category. Modern competitive judo is also fought in different gender and weight groups.

By 1882, Kano had become an instructor at a school for the upper echelons of society and 11 years later, at age 35, he was appointed headmaster of a teachers' training school. For 26 years, Jigoro Kano devoted himself to the development and wellbeing of the teachers under his care at the training school. During this time, he had also established the Kobun Gakuin, which accommodated and instructed foreign students, and the private Kano School, which educated more than 300 young men over the following 40 years.

Initially, the Kodokan was managed entirely by Jigoro Kano, but in 1894 the first consultative body was formed and in 1909 it became a foundation. It was in the same year that Kano became the first Japanese member of the International Olympic Committee (IOC) and, two years later, founded the Japanese Athletic Association, becoming its first president.

JIGORO KANO ESTABLISHED KODOKAN JUDO ON THE BASIC PRINCIPLES UNDERLYING CLASSICAL JUJUTSU TECHNIQUES.

The Kodokan is now the headquarters of the All Japan Judo Federation, the formalized institution that had been established in 1949. The sport's governing body, the International Judo Federation, was formed in 1951 and is presently situated in Seoul in South Korea. Jigoro Kano's eldest daughter, the late Noriko Watanuki, was the head of the Kodokan women's division for many years, and his grandson, Yukimitsu Kano, remains the current president.

On 4 May 1938, Jigoro Kano succumbed to pneumonia and passed away aboard the SS *Hikawa Maru*. He was returning from Cairo where he had attended the IOC meeting nominating Tokyo, Japan, as host of the 12th Olympic Games. By the time of Jigoro Kano's death, the sport of judo had grown to such an extent that there were over 100,000 black-belt practitioners. The present Kodokan in Tokyo was completed in 1982 and, for many *judoka* worldwide, it is a cherished ambition to train there at some point in their career.

SAMURAI WERE MEMBERS OF THE JAPANESE WARRIOR CLASS THAT COMPRISED THE FIGHTING ELITE IN THE FEUDAL PERIOD BETWEEN THE ELEVENTH AND NINETEENTH CENTURIES IN JAPAN.

Judo — a concise explanation

Judo is a martial art that evolved from jujutsu, a form of unarmed combat practised by the Japanese Samurai. As a pupil of the jujutsu schools, Jigoro Kano found that they practised their techniques as a sequential system of prearranged forms as opposed to an interactive free-flowing movement, and thus developed his own interpretation. As a result, Jigoro Kano is often referred to as *Shihan* — a Japanese term for 'master teacher' — and in judo circles, this honorary title belongs to him exclusively.

The *Shihan* considered the prearranged forms as a weakness and began to study ways of applying the techniques in what he called *randori*, or free movement. Through this research, he came to realize that one of the most important skills was that of *kuzushi*, or breaking of balance, which enabled him to throw opponents who were bigger or stronger. The *Shihan* soon realized, however, that the striking techniques were too dangerous to practise during *randori* but he nevertheless retained them in the formal techniques of the *kata*. The primary difference between the movements of *randori* and the movements of *kata* is that the former is freely applied in practice and sparring; and the latter is formal and idealized to illustrate specific combative principles.

Standing judo consists of a variety of techniques that are used to throw a partner to the ground with control. These techniques include the use of the hands, hips, legs and feet. They also include techniques where you sacrifice your own balance and fall to the ground in order to throw your partner. The groundwork techniques in judo are a logical sequential movement from the standing techniques and should not be practised in isolation. They consist of manoeuvres in which you pin your partner on his back, thereby controlling his body so that he cannot escape. In conjunction with pinning techniques, arm locks are also applied in judo but only against the elbow joint in competition.

Because throws are an integral part of the sport of judo, it is vital that you fall correctly without being injured. It is thus equally important that you practise in a designated area. This area is referred to as a *dojo*.

The *dojo* has mats, or *tatami*, that cover the floor for safety. Observing all the safety precautions enables the *judoka* to practise for many years and gain the maximum benefits of the sport without being hurt. The mats are specially manufactured to cushion the fall and are reinforced to absorb the impact. The first judo mats were manufactured from compressed straw and covered with finely woven rush matting, while contemporary mats are made from a compressed synthetic material such as neoprene and are covered with vinyl. All *judoka* wear a *judogi*, or judo suit, that resembles a loose-fitting suit with no buttons or pockets — for safety reasons — and the feet are left bare. The jacket is fastened with a belt that indicates the level of skill of the *judoka*.

Finally, judo is best defined in the words of its founder, Jigoro Kano, who in 1915 stated that judo is 'the way of the highest or maximum efficient use of physical and mental energy'.

AMERICAN SIMON JACKSON IS A VISUALLY IMPAIRED JUDO AND PARALYMPIC CHAMPION.

GETTING STARTED

Judo attire consists of a suit of three parts: the pants, the jacket with reinforced stitching, and the belt, which indicates the proficiency and level of technical skill of the judoka — although this varies from country to country, as each one has its own grading system. The standard entry level for international competition is a black belt. Some countries also have a separate grading system for judo players who are still at school. This is usually linked to the physical education requirements in the schools.

The judo *gi*

In addition to white judo suits, blue judo suits are also worn and were introduced to differentiate between the competitors in international competition. The universally accepted rules stipulate that contestants shall wear judo *gi* complying with the following conditions:

- Strongly made in cotton or similar material, in good condition (without rent or tear). The material must not be so thick or so hard as to prevent the opponent from taking a grip.
- Blue in colour for the first contestant and white or off-white for the second contestant.
- Acceptable markings:
  - National Olympic abbreviation (on the back of the jacket)
  - National Emblem (on left breast of jacket). Maximum size 10cm x 10cm (4in x 4in)
  - Manufacturer's trademark (on bottom-front of jacket and bottom-front of left leg of trousers). Maximum size 5cm x 5cm (2in x 2in)
  - Shoulder markings (from the collar, across shoulder, and down arm on both sides of the jacket). Maximum length 5cm x 5cm (2in x 2in) and maximum width 5cm (2in)
  - Where applicable, indication of the placing (1st, 2nd, 3rd) at the Olympic Games or World Championships, in an area of 6cm x 10cm (2½in x 4in) at the bottom-front left side of the jacket.

left THE STANDARD WHITE *GI*, ALONG WITH THE APPROPRIATELY COLOURED BELT, IS THE CONVENTIONAL ATTIRE FOR BOTH THE DOJO AND THE COMPETITIVE ARENA, WHERE AN OPPONENT MAY WEAR A BLUE *GI* TO DIFFERENTIATE BETWEEN TWO COMPETITORS.
opposite THE COLOUR OF THE JUDOKA'S BELT, RANGING FROM BLACK THROUGH RED-AND-WHITE BLOCKS TO RED, INDICATES THE JUDOKA'S LEVEL OF SKILL.

■ The contestant's name may be worn on the belt, the lower front of the jacket and upper front of the pants. Maximum size 3cm x 10cm (1¹⁄₅in x 4in). Also, the contestant's name or abbreviation may be placed above the National Olympic abbreviation, but may not prevent an opponent from grasping the jacket. There are also a number of additional stipulations as to size and position.

■ The jacket should be long enough to cover the thighs and reach at least to the fists when the arms are fully extended downwards at the sides of the body. The body of the jacket should be worn with the left side crossed over the right and should be wide enough to have a minimum overlap of 20cm (8in) at the level of the bottom of the ribcage. The sleeves of the jacket should reach no further than the wrist joint and may not be shorter than 5cm (2in) above the wrist joint. In addition, there should be a space of 10—15cm (4—6in) between the sleeve and the arm (inclusive of bandages) along the entire length of the sleeve.

■ The trousers, free of any markings, should be long enough to cover the legs and should reach to the ankle joint or be no more than 5cm (2in) above the joint. There should be a space of 10—15cm (4—6in) between the trouser leg and the leg (inclusive of the bandages) along the entire length of the trouser leg.

■ A strong belt, 4—5cm (1¹⁄₂—2in) wide — and the colour must correspond with the participant's grade — should be worn over the jacket at waist level and tied with a square knot, tight enough to prevent the jacket from being too loose and long enough to go twice around the waist, leaving 20—30cm (8—12in) protruding from each side of the knot when the belt has been tied.

■ Female contestants shall wear under the jacket:

■ a strong plain white or off-white T-shirt, with short sleeves and long enough to be worn inside the trousers, or

■ a strong plain white or off-white leotard with short sleeves.

The belt

Junior (Kyu) Grades vary from country to country, but usually start with a white belt progressing to brown belt. Senior (Dan) Grades, as recognized by the International Judo Federation (IJF), are indicated by various belt colours and patterns:

■ 1st Dan to 5th Dan   black belt
■ 6th Dan to 8th Dan   red-and-white blocked belt
■ 9th and 10th Dan   red belt

A black belt may also be worn by 6th to 10th Dan judo players if they wish to do so.

It is important for the knot of the belt to be at the front for safety precautions. If it is at the back and the *judoka* falls backwards onto it, there is the possibility that he or she may be injured.

A   BLACK BELT: 1ST TO 5TH DAN

B   RED-AND-WHITE BLOCKED BELT: 6TH TO 8TH DAN

C   RED BELT: 9TH TO 10TH DAN

Tying the belt

A Hold the belt so that both ends are of equal length, with the belt's middle against your stomach.

B Cross the ends of the belt behind you to form a circle around your body; bring them back to the front.

C Cross the right-hand end over the left and thread it underneath both circles, pulling it up and through.

D Place the left-hand end of the belt over the right-hand end and pull it through.

E Pull both ends of the belt tight.

F Finally, ensure that both ends are of equal length.

Equipment

Referees should have the following equipment:

- A drawsheet showing bout participants
- A judo scoreboard
- A red belt and a white belt
- Six flags (three blue and three white) to indicate a *hantei* or decision
- Two stopwatches by which to keep time
- A buzzer (or bell)
- Three flags for the referees' table:
    - Blue: Hold being timed
    - Green: No timing taking place
    - Yellow: Injury being timed

The *tatami*

The *tatami* (judo mat) must be thick enough to cushion the impact of a break fall. At international competitions, the mat must be at least 45mm (1³⁄₄in) thick, 8m (26ft) wide, with a 1m (3¹⁄₃ft) red danger area and a 3m (9ft) safety area. Smaller mat areas are permissible for training, depending on the *dojo* size.

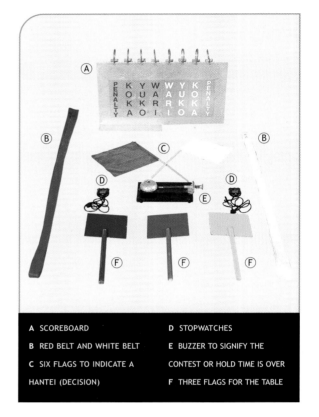

A SCOREBOARD	**D** STOPWATCHES
B RED BELT AND WHITE BELT	**E** BUZZER TO SIGNIFY THE
C SIX FLAGS TO INDICATE A	CONTEST OR HOLD TIME IS OVER
HANTEI (DECISION)	**F** THREE FLAGS FOR THE TABLE

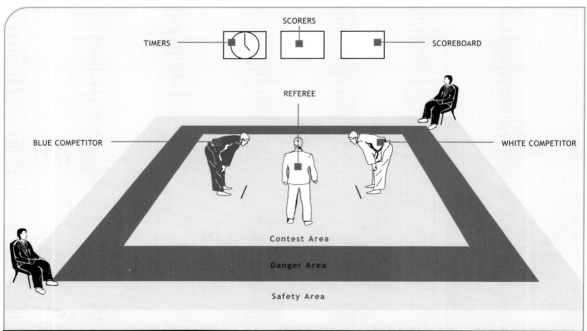

ALTHOUGH THE DIMENSIONS OF THE *TATAMI* MAY VARY SLIGHTLY ACCORDING TO THE DOJO AND COMPETITIVE ENVIRONMENT, THE SQUARE SAFETY AREA IS GENERALLY 14–16M (46–52FT), INCORPORATING A CONTEST AREA OF 8–10M (26–33FT) AND A DANGER AREA OF 1M (3FT).

Hygiene

Because judoka work in such close contact with each other, personal hygiene and specific personal habits are important, not only for health reasons but also for the purposes of safety.

- Long hair should always be tied back neatly.
- Jewellery should not be worn at all, as it could hurt either you or your partner/opponent. For example, earrings could be accidentally pulled out.
- Feet and hands should be clean and nails should be kept short.
- Ensure that wounds are well covered.
- Sandals should be worn to and from the judo mat to keep your feet and the mat as clean as possible.
- Do not eat for half an hour prior to training.
- Do not train if you are ill. This is not only dangerous for you, but you risk spreading the illness among your fellow students.

If you are taking medication, consult your doctor prior to any form of training or competition, as it could be dangerous to exercise while on certain types of medication. In addition, certain substances in medication are prohibited under International Judo Federation competition rules. Your doctor should have access to the list of prohibited substances.

Judo safety

Beginners should never train without the supervision of a qualified judo instructor, as unsupervised and untutored judo techniques can be potentially dangerous. Always ensure that judo mats are used when practising to avoid injury.

Ensure that you only practise judo with someone who is able to fall correctly. The practice area must always be safe so make sure that tables and chairs are moved away from the mat area, and that there are no sharp objects on or around the mat that could cause injury. Always ensure that you are able to contact someone, either by telephone or someone in the immediate area, who is able to administer first aid in the case of an emergency. By taking careful note of all the safety precautions, you can avoid injuries that may occur in contact sports such as judo.

Approach to training

As in all the martial arts, a student's personal approach to training is one of the most important elements. It is always important to be attentive and listen to your judo teacher. By listening, not only can you gain the maximum benefit from your classes, but it may also be vital to your safety.

Because a successful judo throw is based on the principle of breaking balance, your teacher is in the position to observe and evaluate all the aspects of the attempt. Even some aspect or detail that may appear insignificant, might make the difference between a throw being successful or putting yourself in a position where you may be thrown by your opponent.

Always treat your training partner with the respect and care that you would expect to receive, because without training partners, you would not be able to practise and acquire the necessary skill to master each technique successfully.

DISCIPLINE, AND RESPECT FOR YOUR OPPONENT AND TEACHER ARE BEST LEARNT FROM AN EARLY AGE.

Bowing in Judo

Bowing in judo today has no religious significance. It is simply a mark of respect to your fellow *judoka*, coach and opponents. By bowing, you are essentially saying 'Please will you work with me' at the beginning, and 'Thank you for working with me' at the end of the practice or competition. This is a common courtesy, and is an important part of judo, as it develops respect for your fellow *judoka*. It is a courtesy to bow to your teacher or coach when requesting assistance or asking permission to leave the training area.

These displays of respect all help develop a sense of discipline and camaraderie in the class. As illustrated below, there are two types of bowing in judo.

A The bow is done from a standing position. Stand with your heels together and your feet slightly apart, with the palms of your hands flat against your sides.

B When bowing, move your hands from the sides to the front of the thighs; at the same time lean forward to approximately 30°. Finish bowing by moving your hands back to your sides as you straighten up.

C You may also bow from the kneeling position. Kneel on the mat with the upper part of both feet flat and with the big toes touching. Your hands rest on the top of your thighs with your buttocks on your heels and your back held as straight and upright as possible.

D To bow, place the palms of both hands on the mat with the fingertips touching. Your elbows must be close to your body. Lean forward so that your back is level while keeping your buttocks on your heels. When you are finished bowing return to the starting position.

Submission

Submission in judo is the indication by one player to another that the player submitting concedes the advantage and the technique being applied must immediately stop.

Due to the very nature of combative sports such as judo, it is necessary to be able to submit — be it simply on the practice mat or in the competitive arena, and it is essential that both participants adhere strictly to the rule of submission.

To submit in judo, firmly tap the mat or your partner's body with the palm of your hand. If you are unable to use your hands in order to indicate submission, you may do so by tapping with your foot on the ground or saying '*Maitta*'.

The participant on whom the technique is applied should submit as soon as he or she is able to feel that the technique is working or if he/she is in any physical pain. To avoid injury, the person who is applying the technique — in other words, the participant who has gained the upper hand in the bout — must immediately stop and release the partner as soon as he or she indicates submission.

WITH THE PALM OF YOUR HAND, TAP EITHER YOUR PARTNER OR THE MAT AT LEAST TWICE TO SIGNAL A SUBMISSION.

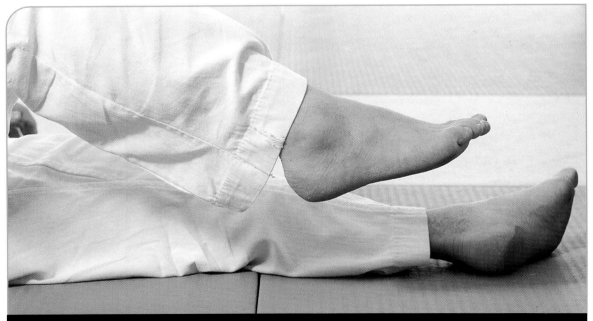

IF YOUR HANDS ARE TRAPPED, YOU ARE STILL ABLE TO SUBMIT BY TAPPING THE MAT WITH EITHER OF YOUR FEET.

Stretching and warming up

Because judo is a contact sport characterized by sudden bursts of energy, you need to develop a supple body. Correct stretching will help minimize the chance of injury to muscles, ligaments and joints.

As a basic rule, stretching should be done slowly with gradual increases in effort. Stretching exercises should be done prior to training.

The warm-up

Warm-up is done after stretching and before commencing with training or competition. It should be done in such a way as to slowly increase your heart and respiratory rate. The exercises should be based on the movements you will use in judo as these will help develop skill at the same time.

Your coach will advise correct warm-up techniques for your age and physical condition. Your level of fitness should increase gradually if you follow a regular training programme. If you are injured, follow medical advice and avoid the temptation to return to training before you have fully recovered. The careers of many *judoka* have been cut short by compounding injuries.

A SKYWARD STRETCH: WITH YOUR HANDS TOGETHER, STRETCH TOWARD THE CEILING.

B SHOULDER STRETCH 1: BRING YOUR ARM ACROSS THE FRONT OF YOUR BODY AND PLACE IT IN THE BEND OF THE OTHER ARM.

C SHOULDER STRETCH 2: STRETCH YOUR ARMS OUT BEHIND YOU AND CLASP YOUR HANDS. LIFT, BUT DO NOT BEND FORWARD.

D LUNGE: STRETCH ONE LEG OUT BEHIND YOU WHILE FACING FORWARD, KEEPING YOUR HEELS GROUNDED. DON'T TURN TO THE SIDE.

E–F HEAD ROLL: TILT YOUR EAR TOWARDS YOUR SHOULDER, KEEPING BOTH SHOULDERS RELAXED. REPEAT ON THE OTHER SIDE.

G ALL-FOURS: PLACE YOUR FEET WIDE APART, KEEPING THE SOLES FLAT ON THE FLOOR. KEEPING YOUR BACK STRAIGHT, PLACE YOUR PALMS FLAT ON THE FLOOR.

H SITTING STRETCH: FROM A SITTING POSITION, BEND ONE LEG FORWARD. REACH FORWARD AND HOLD YOUR TOES.

I INNER-THIGH STRETCH: SITTING ON BOTH BUTTOCKS, HOLD YOUR TOES AND BREATHE IN DEEPLY. AS YOU EXHALE, PRESS YOUR KNEES TOWARD THE FLOOR.

FALLING

Learning to fall correctly is a key skill in judo as it reduces the risk of injury. In addition, confident *judoka* will steadily improve their overall skills when they are not afraid of falling, as they will be able to try new techniques without being injured.

This ability to fall correctly and safely is also important from a self-defence point of view, because if you are thrown to the ground unexpectedly, your ability to fall correctly will save you from injury and thus enable you to fight back or even escape. The most important parts of the body to protect when falling are the head, neck and base of the spine.

Ukemi (Breakfalls)

Ukemi, or breakfalls, are not only a way of falling safely, but are also an important way to strengthen the muscles of the body, which in turn helps cushion the body against the shock of the fall.

The continuous practice of *ukemi* achieves this through the striking action of the arms and legs when you are being thrown, or when you practise falling techniques. This extends to the muscles of the back and, through the correct practice of keeping your head tucked in when falling, helps to develop and strengthen the neck muscles.

This also has enormous benefits to groundwork as it allows you to keep your head tucked in to protect your neck, thus preventing your opponent's hands and arms from reaching under your chin to apply strangleholds around your neck. It also helps you to recover quickly when you fall or are thrown to the ground in a self-defence scenario.

Having mastered the *ukemi*, you will also be more confident to attack in *randori* (see page 13) because you will have less fear of being thrown.

Ukemi also allows you to help less experienced *judoka* learn their throwing techniques as you will be less likely to suffer injury when being thrown.

Common injury sites during breakfalls

BACK OF THE HEAD

BASE OF THE NECK

SMALL OF THE BACK

LUMBAR REGION

COCCYX

left THE HEAD, NECK AND BASE OF THE SPINE ARE PARTICULARLY SUSCEPTIBLE TO INJURY DURING A FALL. TO AVOID SERIOUS INJURIES TO THESE BODY AREAS, *JUDOKA* NEED TO PAY SPECIAL ATTENTION TO THE CORRECT FALLING TECHNIQUES.

opposite THE ABILITY TO FALL CORRECTLY WILL NOT ONLY REDUCE THE RISK OF INJURY, BUT WILL ADD TO THE *JUDOKA*'S PERFORMANCE.

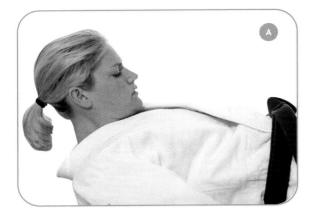

The basics of falling

⇐ When learning to fall, you should start in the lowest possible position so as to build confidence in the falling technique. The most important criterion when falling backwards is the position of the head. Your chin should be tucked in towards your chest and your eyes firmly focused on the knot of your belt. In the beginning, you may find this difficult but, with practice, your neck muscles will develop, enabling you to hold this position with ease.

⇒ Another important element of falling backwards is the position of the hands and arms when striking the mat with your back. Your arms should strike the mat at 45° to your body so that the palms of your hands and the muscles of your forearm hit the mat. When practising this in the lying position, your knees should be bent so that the base of your spine is raised off the mat.

⇐ In order to best cushion your body from the impact of falling on your side, the impact is taken on the outside of the thigh muscles with your head again tucked in to your chest and arms striking the mat at 45°. Do not strike the mat with the heel of your foot, but rather with the inside of the foot, and the knee of the leg taking the impact should be slightly bent.

Backward breakfall

⇧ From a sitting position, prior to rolling backwards to strike the mat with both arms, hold both arms out in front of you with your legs straight and your feet slightly apart. Ensure that your head is tucked in with your chin on your chest.

⇧ Roll backwards while keeping your chin firmly against your chest. Raise your legs up in the air with your hips off the mat. As your shoulders touch the mat, strike the mat with the muscles of the forearms and the palms of both hands.

⇧ Once you have mastered the ability to fall from the sitting position, you will need to progress to the next level of falling. Start in the squatting position and step backwards with your left foot. Sit with your buttocks on the heel of your left foot, keeping your chin tucked firmly down on your chest. Roll onto your back again, lifting your legs into the air, and strike the mat with both arms.

⇦ ⇧ To fall from a standing position, stand with your feet slightly apart, your chin firmly against your chest and arms extended in front of you. Step back with your left foot and sit with your buttocks towards the heel of your left foot. As your buttocks touch your left foot, roll onto your back, keeping your head tucked in. Allow the momentum to lift your legs and hips into the air while striking the mat firmly with both arms.

Side breakfall

⇧ To start the side breakfall, begin in the squatting position with both arms extended in front of you and your chin on your chest.

⇧ From this position, extend your left leg forward and swing it across to your right. As you do this, roll onto your left side.

⇧ Strike the mat with the fore-arm and palm of your left hand, raising your hips and legs into the air. Practise falling to the right too.

⇨ To fall from a standing position to the left-hand side, hold the belt knot with your right hand, while swinging the left leg forwards and across in front of your right leg.

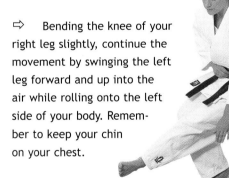

⇨ Bending the knee of your right leg slightly, continue the movement by swinging the left leg forward and up into the air while rolling onto the left side of your body. Remember to keep your chin on your chest.

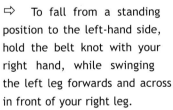

⇦ As the side of your buttock begins to touch the surface of the mat, raise your left arm up in the air, while continuing to roll onto your left side.

⇦ As momentum carries you onto your side, strike the mat with your left palm and forearm at about 45˚ to the side of your body. Keep your head tucked in while lifting your hips and legs. Practise to both the left and right.

Falling forward by rolling

The rolling action in judo differs from gymnastics in that the impact is taken across the shoulders from the back of the shoulder to the opposite hip. At no time should the head or neck touch the mat.

⇨　To start, stand with your feet apart, with your right leg forward. Place both hands on the mat, with the right hand slightly forward and to the inside of the right foot. Place the left hand close to the right hand, with the fingers of the right and left hands pointing towards one another. Tuck your head in and place your chin close to your chest. Your palms must lie flat on the mat.

⇦　Push out with both legs and roll forward over your right shoulder, keeping your head tucked in to your chest. The roll should be across the back of the right shoulder towards the left hip.

⇨　While allowing your forward momentum to roll you over onto the outer edge of your left side, left hip and left thigh, strike the mat firmly with your left arm. Your feet should be apart, with both the right and left legs held straight. If you have gained sufficient momentum, you will continue the roll up onto your feet.

Front break

The action of falling forward is used when spinning out of throwing attacks or when you are unable to execute a rolling break fall.

⇦ Start the forward roll from the kneeling position, with your body upright. Raise both arms in front of you, with the palms of your hands facing forward and your arms slightly bent.

From a kneeling position

⇨ Fall forward from the knees. Strike the mat with your forearms and palms, keeping the elbows bent. Look up towards the ceiling but keep your back slightly arched. Do not allow your chest or stomach to touch the mat. Only the underside of your toes should be in contact with the mat.

⇦ Again raise both arms with elbows bent and the palms facing away. As you fall, throw both feet backward so that you land on the forearms and toes with your body off the mat.

From a standing position

⇨ Stand with your feet apart and your arms forward and slightly bent. Then lean forward, keeping your body straight.

⇩ As you fall, throw both legs backward so that you land on your forearms and the bottom of the toes, with your feet apart and your knees and body clear of the mat.

Spinning out forwards

It is possible to escape from throwing techniques if you are able to break your opponent's control by twisting out of the throwing action. You should land in a position where your opponent cannot score points for the technique. This is usually done by turning away from your opponent's attacking leg. To learn how to do this, you should first practise onto a crash mat or similar soft surface. The most important element to remember in these turning actions is to pay special attention to the turning action of your head and to avoid landing on your side or back.

⇦   Start with your feet wide apart in the standing position. Raise both arms as if you are doing a forward breakfall from a standing position (see page 30). Rotate your shoulders and your head while keeping your feet still so that you are now looking behind you.

⇦   Continue the rotation while falling forward, but remember to keep your arms close to your body. Do not extend your arms as you could lock both elbows and injure yourself.

⇨   Complete the turn and the falling action so that you land on your forearms and toes with your chest clear of the mat.

Spinning out backwards

Much like the equivalent forward motion (see page 31), you may also escape throwing techniques by twisting out in a backward movement.

⇨ You may use the twisting out action against a foot sweep. In this way, the defender (white) is able to break loose from the opponent's (blue) control of his arms.

⇦ By turning faster than the throwing action — and in the same direction as the original attack — the defender is able to rotate away from his opponent and escape to land on his front.

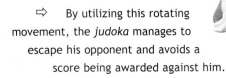

⇨ By utilizing this rotating movement, the *judoka* manages to escape his opponent and avoids a score being awarded against him.

Spinning out from throws

Spinning-out actions have become a very important facet of modern competitive judo. Due to the speed of the attacks, it is vital that a *judoka* learns at an early stage how to rotate out of the opponent's attacking movements, as there may not be sufficient time to block them. These rotating actions, executed while breaking your opponent's control, also help prevent your opponent scoring the maximum points for throwing techniques, thereby giving you a chance to continue fighting — and possibly win.

Osoto gari (Large outer reap)

When your opponent attempts to reap or hook your right leg with his right leg, you will be able to turn away from his attacking leg to land on the front of your body by rotating your body away from his attacking leg. This is possible while balancing on your left leg, ducking your head under his right arm and breaking his control of your right arm. Remember to turn your head as fast as possible in the direction in which you turn.

Ouchi gari (Large inner reap)

As your opponent attempts to reap your left leg on the inside with his right leg, rotate your body towards the right and, while pulling your right arm loose, continue to turn your head to the right so that you fall onto your stomach instead of onto your back.

Kouchi gari (Small inner reap)

As your opponent tries to reap your right leg from the inside with his right foot, lift your right foot and rotate your body sharply to the left, while breaking his control on your left collar. Turn to land on your stomach.

IN A COMPETITIVE SCENARIO, THE *JUDOKA* SPINNING OUT OF THE *OUCHI-GARI* (LEFT) MAY BE ABLE TO AVERT THE POSSIBLE *IPPON* TO A LESSER SCORE FOR THE OPPONENT (RIGHT).

GROUNDWORK

Groundwork, or grappling, is an integral feature of judo, and it is very important not to lose sight of the link between standing techniques and groundwork. A well-trained *judoka* will be equally skilled in both. Mastery of ground (or grappling) techniques will enable you to attack with confidence from a standing position as you will have no fear of being brought to the ground should your throwing technique be unsuccessful. This will also give you the opportunity to apply groundwork techniques. Take-downs are not standard throws in judo but are designed specifically to bring your opponent to the ground so that you can apply a hold, arm lock or strangle.

Grappling techniques

Grappling techniques, or *katame waza*, in judo are divided into three distinct groups:

- *osaekomi waza* (pinning or hold-downs)
- *shime waza* (strangulation techniques)
- *kansetsu waza* (joint techniques or arm locks).

The latter two techniques are particularly effective in a self-defence situation, but not when facing more than one opponent

Osaekomi waza (Hold-downs)

Osaekomi waza, or hold-downs, are techniques in which you pin your opponent down — mainly on his or her back. These holds are usually executed from the side, the top, or astride your opponent. The strangulation and arm lock techniques in judo enable you to win a contest even when you are being pinned in a hold. This is one of the distinct differences between wrestling and judo — a *judoka* is able to fight back and win by using a strangle or arm lock, even when being pinned on the ground.

The referee will announce *osaekomi* when, in his or her opinion, the applied technique corresponds with the following criteria:

- The contestant being held must be controlled by his opponent and must have his back and one or both shoulders in contact with the mat.
- The control can be made from the side, from the rear or from on top.
- The contestant applying the hold must not have his leg(s) or body controlled by his opponent's legs.
- At least one of the contestants has any part of his body touching the contest area at the announcement by the referee of *osaekomi*.
- The contestant applying the hold must have his body in either the *kesa* (see page 36) or the *shiho* (see page 37) position — in other words, similar techniques to *kesa gatame* (scarf hold) or *kami shiho gatame* (upper four-corner hold).

Shime waza (Strangulation techniques)

In competitive judo, strangles are applied using the various parts of the body or the judo *gi*. Competitors may not, however, wrap any part of the judo *gi* around any part of their opponent's body. Pressure may also not be applied to the trachea, or windpipe.

If executed correctly, the strangle will cut off blood flow and air supply — but only enough so that the opponent is able to submit and does not pass out.

Kansetsu waza (Arm locks)

Kansetsu waza are techniques where pressure is applied to the elbow joint, thereby forcing your opponent's submission — one of the techniques you can use when being pinned on the ground. There are locks applied to other joints in judo, but these are not used in competition.

opposite A WELL-TRAINED *JUDOKA* WILL NOT ONLY BE PROFICIENT IN ESTABLISHED STANDING TECHNIQUES, BUT WILL ALSO HAVE MASTERED THE SKILL OF WELL-EXECUTED GROUNDWORK.

↘ Kesa gatame (Scarf hold)

Pin your opponent on her back, with the right side of your chest pressing against the right side of her chest, while holding her right arm as tightly as possible under your left arm with your right arm around her neck. This method of holding your opponent down by using your bodyweight and the control of her arm, makes it very difficult for her to escape. She has to use all her strength and body movement to free her right arm before she can begin to escape. When executing this hold, it is important to keep your body relaxed while maintaining control over your opponent's arm and head. Your legs should be as wide apart as possible, with your right leg forward, your left leg back and your knees slightly bent. At the same time, however, you must be extremely careful not to allow your opponent to hook her legs around your legs, as this will allow her to control the movement of your body. This will also make it easier for your opponent to free her right arm by turning her body towards you and using the twisting action of her body to pull her right arm loose. Remember that the secret to this hold is the control of your opponent's arm and body by the effective use of your chest and weight in pinning her down on the mat.

⇐ Kuzure kesa gatame (Modified scarf hold)

Starting in the same position as you would in *kesa gatame* (above), control your opponent's right arm by pinning it underneath your left armpit, holding the arm firmly with your left hand. However, instead of placing your right arm around your opponent's neck, place it underneath her left armpit and your elbow tight against her body. As your opponent attempts to escape by rolling you over her body, move your right hand out from underneath her armpit and place it on the mat to prevent her turning you over. The key points to remember in this hold are the tight control of your opponent's right arm and to lock her body against you with your right arm by pulling your elbow and your arm in tightly against her body, wedging her body in against you while holding her.

⇧ **Tate shiho gatame (Astride seating)**

In the *tate shiho gatame*, or astride seating, sit astride your opponent with one leg situated on each side of her body with your weight on your knees. Hook both feet in underneath your opponent's thighs, thus enabling you to control her body to prevent her turning you over. Place your right arm around your opponent's neck while, at the same time, placing her right arm between your head and her head. Pin her arm tightly between your head and her head by pushing your body forward and down against the arm. Your right hand should be locked firmly around her neck.

⇧ Your left hand helps control her right arm, but your hand must be able to move freely. If your opponent tries to bridge and roll you towards your left, your left hand can block her. If your opponent tries to bridge and roll you towards your right, throw your weight towards your left shoulder, blocking her rolling action. The important points in this hold are controlling your opponent's legs with your legs, controlling her shoulder and arm with your head, and distributing your weight by pitching your body forward firmly onto your opponent's shoulders while maintaining control with your legs.

⇩ **Kata gatame (Shoulder-holding)**

Hold your opponent on her back by pinning her right arm across the front of her neck with your shoulder and your head. Start in the *kesa gatame*, or scarf hold, position. When your opponent frees her right arm and pushes under your chin with her right hand, push her right arm across in front of her head towards the left. Lower your head and, with the right side of your head and the top of your right shoulder, pin her right arm firmly across in front of her neck. Keep your right arm around the back of her neck and place your left hand in your right hand. Bring your right

knee up into her side so that your weight is on your right knee. Extend your left leg to the side, keeping it straight so that you form a triangle between your hands, right knee and left foot. Lowering your hips, maintain your balance and push your weight forward onto her right shoulder. Remember to keep your right knee tight against your opponent's body with your foot off the ground and your weight on your toes. Your left foot must be firmly on the mat with the sole touching the mat. Control your opponent's right arm and shoulder by applying pressure, using your neck and shoulder. If you maintain this control and she cannot free her right arm, it will be very difficult for her to escape.

⇧ Kami shiho gatame
(Upper four-corner hold)

Kneel or lean on your opponent's shoulders with both knees to the right of your opponent's head. Place your left arm underneath her left shoulder and take hold of her belt, with your thumb inside the belt. Place your right arm underneath your opponent's right shoulder and again take hold of her belt. Place your weight firmly forward onto her chest, head toward the left, legs outstretched. Move your feet apart and, while maintaining firm control with both hands, pull her in tight against your chest. Your weight should be firmly distributed across her chest, with your feet wide apart and your toes on the mat. The key to this hold is to move freely with your opponent as she moves, so that you maintain the same position on top of her head. If your opponent attempts to bridge (see page 39) to escape, pull her towards you with both hands so that she cannot balance on her shoulders — this will make it difficult for her to bridge.

⇩ Yoko shiho gatame
(Side four-quarter hold)

Kneel at right angles to your opponent's body when she is lying on her back. If you are kneeling against her right side, place your left hand underneath her neck and take firm control of her left collar with your left hand. Place your chest firmly on your opponent's chest with your right hand between her legs, underneath her left leg, and taking hold of her belt or the bottom of her jacket.

Lie flat on your stomach (see below) with both your legs behind you and your feet as wide as possible. Arch your back and push down onto your opponent's body with your chest. The arching of your back lowers your hips and makes it difficult for your opponent to turn underneath you or to place her legs underneath your body. Pull her lightly in against your chest with both hands. If your opponent tries to use her left hand to push against your head, turn your head to look towards her legs while lowering your head, but maintain the arched position of your body so that you wedge your opponent against your chest. Do not lift your hips, as this will enable your opponent to move her legs underneath you to help her roll you over.

The bridge

One of the most important escapes in judo is the bridge. This action uses the leg and back muscles, combined with the arms, to obtain maximum power in rolling your opponent over or pushing her away.

⇦ You should bridge on your shoulders with your back clear of the mat and your heels close to your buttocks, with your knees bent, as this will give you maximum power when pushing your legs.

⇨ To start the turn, place your weight on the top corner of your left shoulder, and continue the movement by bringing your right leg up and over your left leg, while maintaining the bridging action.

↗ Rotate your hips to the left and keep turning over until you end up on your stomach. Practise this movement to both sides, until it is a smooth and continuous action. Remember to bridge towards the top of the shoulders and do not just roll sideways. It is important to use the power of the legs, back and arm muscles at the same time or you will not be able to create a space in which to turn your hips. The rotation of the hips generates the power you will require for the turning action. While you are being held from the top of your body, escape by bridging. Maintain the bridge and walk with your feet to the right before rotating to the left. Reverse this action when you wish to rotate to the right. The walking action again creates a space in which to turn and also helps break your opponent's balance.

Escaping from holds

Kesa gatame (Scarf hold)

⇨ You can use the bridge against a scarf hold. Note the strong rotation of your body onto the side to loosen the right arm, before you begin the bridge action.

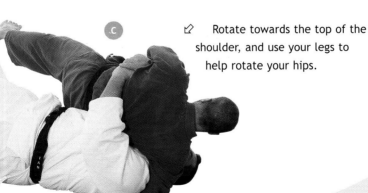

⇦ In the bridging action, your opponent (blue) is locked onto your chest, with his balance broken toward his head.

⇗ Rotate towards the top of the shoulder, and use your legs to help rotate your hips.

⇨ To complete the escape, the opponent should be turned almost completely over the top of your left shoulder. As the movement is continued, you will be in a strong attacking position, having rolled him over your body and onto his back. You must take tight control with your hands before you start.

Yoko shiho gatame (Side four-quarter hold)

When your opponent holds you in the side four-quarters, first rotate your body onto your side — towards your opponent — so you can hook your left leg over your opponent's head if you are being held from the right.

⇨ In order to rotate your body onto your side and hook your leg over, push against the left side of your opponent's head with the palm of your left hand, and hook your left leg over his head.

⇨ Once you have managed to hook your leg over his head, you can now cross your legs, with your left foot hooked into the bend of your right leg.

⇨ Continue to push with your legs — this is the start of the stranglehold — with your opponent's neck and shoulder locked between your legs. At this point, the hold is broken in competition judo. By taking hold of your opponent's belt with your left hand, and pushing with your right hand underneath his hip, you can now lift his body — and if you then rotate your body to the left and continue to roll, your opponent will be rolled over you, with you ending up in a strong holding position.

Kami shiho gatame (Upper four-quarters hold)

⇨   In order to escape from *kami shiho gatame*, or the upper four-quarter hold, you will need to use a bridging action.

⇦   Take hold of your opponent's belt with both hands, with the palm of the hands facing up, and your fingers inside your partner's belt.

⇦   A strong grip on your opponent's belt will enable you to push up against the belt to help lift his weight off your chest. Bridge by bringing your heels in close to your buttocks and lifting up onto your shoulders. Maintaining the bridge (see left), move both feet to the right and then rotate your hips to the left by bringing your left leg over your right leg, and pushing your opponent's weight off your chest with both hands.

⇨   Continue to rotate while keeping your opponent pushed away — this will roll your opponent onto his back, putting you into position to counter the attack with a similar hold.

Tate shiho gatame
(Straight four-corner hold
or astride seating)

⇐ In this escape, use the hooking action of the legs combined with the bridge.

⇐ Push your opponent's right leg with your left hand, so that you can straighten your own leg to unhook it.

⇐ Hook your leg around the outside of your opponent's right leg, maintaining control of his leg. Then bridge and turn to your left side, continuing to roll to the left. Remember that the bridge is not just to the side, but also to the top of your left shoulder.

⇐ Your hands must work together to pull your opponent over. Continue the turning action until you are able to turn your opponent on his back. You are now in a good position to counter his attack.

Using your legs

In judo, your legs are used in a variety of ways to control your opponent in both attack and defence. The following are examples of how to use your legs to the best advantage — as well as some basic escapes.

✍ Control from underneath

If you are on your back and your opponent is between your legs, you can control his body by pulling his head down and locking your feet behind his back. The purpose of the leg action is to gather your opponent towards you so that you are able to restrict his movement. When this is successfully done in a competition, the referee will stop the contest and both contestants will return to the starting positions and continue from there. You should never lock your feet and straighten your legs in a scissor-like action as this is not only dangerous to your opponent, but also illegal and will also incur a penalty during competitions.

⇧ Control from above with turnover

Your opponent is on his hands and knees. Sit astride his belt, hook your feet between his legs, and lean your upper body forward so your weight is directed towards his arms. Your legs should keep you from tipping forward. Drop one shoulder to the ground, keeping your chest against his back, while the leg on the opposite side to the shoulder you dropped to the ground pulls up and around, drawing his leg along with it.

⇧
It is at this rather vital point in the manoeuvre that your hands then come into play, securing your opponent's upper body while your legs continue to exercise control of the lower part of his body by pulling his knees apart.

⇩ Escaping over your opponent's legs

From between your opponent's legs, bring your hands forward to hold onto his belt and then push his legs apart using your elbows.

A With your left hand, take hold of his pants on the inside just above his knee and push his leg to the floor; bring your right leg forward and kneel across his thigh.

B With your left hand, hold his right arm, placing your right arm around his neck as you bring your left leg forward, out from between his legs.

C Bring your right leg forward under your left leg into a splits position and lower your hips while pushing his body with your chest. This can also be done on the opposite side.

⇩ Escaping under your opponent's legs

A Raise your arm, pushing his leg onto your shoulder and push down with your chest; reach across with your left hand and hold his right lapel.

B Move your right leg over your left and then drop your hips. Let go with your right hand, rotate to the left so your right hand is above his shoulder and you are chest to chest.

C Slide your right hand under his head. Move your left hand from his collar to his sleeve, split your legs so your right leg is by his head and your left by his legs.

Mastering the turnover

There are many ways to turn a partner over so that you can apply a hold, strangle or arm lock. Below and over-leaf are examples of basic turnovers. Most turnovers are performed when your opponent is either on his hands and knees or flat on his stomach.

Turnover from the Side (1)

↗ Kneel on the right side of your opponent. Reach under his right armpit and behind his neck with your right hand, lifting his arm as you push your arm through. Your left shoulder should be against his side with your head resting on his back.

⇨ Push with your shoulder off your knees so that your opponent is rotated onto his back, but maintain contact at all times, finishing with your opponent on his back and you with your chest on his chest to hold him.

Turnover from the side (2)

⇦ Start by kneeling on the right side of your opponent, as before. With your left hand, reach under his right armpit and take hold of his opposite lapel (the left lapel). With your right hand, reach in front of his hands and take hold of his left sleeve at the wrist. Place your left shoulder against his right side and turn your head so that your left cheek is against his back.

⇧ With your right hand, pull his left hand forward and push forward with your shoulder.

⇧ Your opponent will collapse onto his back; follow him and proceed into a hold.

From the head

⇨ Kneel in front of your opponent with your chest on the back of his neck. With your left hand, take hold of the sleeve — at the wrist — of his right arm.

⇦ Your right hand should take hold of your opponent's lapel under his armpit. Straighten your left leg and begin to rotate your body to the left, bringing your left leg over your right in a twisting motion.

⇦ Continue to rotate until your chest is resting on his shoulders.

⇨ Finish by locking his left arm to his body with your right arm, and then tuck his right hand under your left armpit and clamp it there, with your chest resting on his chest.

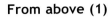

From above (1)
⇐ Okuri eri jime (Sliding collar strangle)

Start the sliding collar strangle by sitting astride your opponent, with your left hand under his left armpit and your right holding his left collar so that your wrist lies against his throat.

⇨ Turn your partner over to the right (see Using your legs on page 44). Your hands secure the opponent's upper body while your legs control the lower part of his body by pulling his knees apart.

⇐ Continue to turn until you are on your back with your partner facing upward, but be sure to maintain control with your legs. With your right hand, reach across and pull down on his left collar while your left hand keeps hold of his right collar to apply the strangulation technique.

From above (2)
⇦ Juji gatame (Cross arm lock)

Start by standing astride your opponent and, with your right hand, reach under his armpit and take hold of the left side of his collar with your thumb inside. Using your left hand, with four fingers inside the collar, push the back of his collar against his head. Curl your left leg over his shoulder so that your leg is between his head and shoulder. Pull up hard with your right hand so that his body turns and is trapped between your legs; then lift your left foot towards your right knee.

⇨ Sit on your opponent and lean back, keeping tight control of his body with your arms and legs.

⇦ As you land on the ground, bring your left leg over your opponent's head. Lock your knees together to control your opponent's arm and shoulder. With both hands, take hold of his hand/wrist so that his thumb is pointing away from you. Pull his arm down to your chest and lift your hips until your opponent submits.

Mastering the strangle

From behind
⇐ Hadaka jime (Naked strangle)

Kneel astride your opponent's belt with your feet tucked against his body. With both hands, reach back and take hold of his pants at his knees, lift up his legs and slide your feet under his upper thighs. This can also be done one leg at a time.

⇐ Let go of your opponent's legs and lean forward so that your hips bear down against his back. If this manoeuvre is done correctly, his legs should come off the ground and his chin should lift up, clearing a path for you to slide your hand under his chin.

⇨ Push your right hand through under his chin and clasp your left hand. Your left hand should be resting on his left shoulder with your forearm down his back. Place your right shoulder against the back of his head and pull back with your left elbow to apply the strangulation technique.

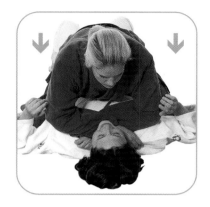

From the front
⇦ Nami juji jime (Cross-handed strangle)

Sit astride your opponent with knees and feet tucked against her side. With your right hand, take hold of her collar on the same side and pull down. With your left hand, take hold of the same collar above your right hand with your thumb inside, and slide your left hand up to her neck so that your hand is under her ear. Let go with your right hand, cross over left and take hold of the opposite collar — also with your thumb inside. Pull tight and place your elbows on the ground to apply the strangulation.

⇦ Kata juji jime (Half cross-handed strangle)

Sit astride your opponent with your knees and feet tucked against her side. With your right hand, take hold of your opponent's collar on the same side and pull down. With your left hand, take hold of the same collar above your right hand, with four fingers inside, and slide your left hand up towards her neck so that your hand is under her ear. Let go with your right hand, cross over left and take hold of the opposite collar, with your thumb inside. Pull with your left hand and try to position your right elbow on the ground so that you are able to apply the strangulation technique.

⇧ Gyaku juji jime (Reverse cross strangle)

Sit astride your opponent with your knees and feet tucked against her side. With your right hand, hold her collar on the same side and pull down. With your left hand, take hold of the same collar above your right hand, with four fingers inside, and slide your left hand up to her neck so your hand is under her ear. Let go with your right hand, cross over left and take hold of the opposite collar also with four fingers inside.

⇧ Holding your opponent tight against you, roll over so that you are on your back with your opponent between your legs. Push down, maintain control with your legs, and pull your elbows outwards as you turn your hands towards each other in order to apply the strangulation technique.

⇧ Kataha jime (Single-wing strangle)

Your opponent is with her back to you, trying to get into a holding position. With your left hand, reach around her neck and take hold of the opposite lapel; use your right hand to feed it to your left if required.

With your right hand, curl it under your opponent's right arm and behind her head — the back of your hand must be against her head. Keep your right arm stiff and push it down, past your opponent's head, while pulling on the left hand to apply the strangulation technique.

⇦ Okuri eri jime (Sliding collar strangle)

You are behind your opponent with your legs controlling her body. With your left hand, reach under her left arm, take hold of her left lapel, and pull it downwards to tighten it.

Now reach around her head and under her chin with your right hand and take hold of her left lapel as high up as possible (left). Let go with your left hand and take hold of her right lapel, pulling down with your left hand and up and across with your right to apply the strangulation technique. This technique can also be executed when your opponent is facing downwards or lying on her side.

⇨ **Sankanku jime (Triangular strangle)**

Your opponent is holding you in *yoko shiho gatame* on your right side. Place your left hand on the side of her neck so that your thumb is just below the ear and push her head down towards your feet.

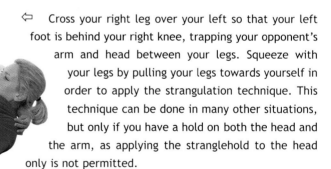

⇨ Bring your left leg up and around to hook it over your opponent's head.

⇦ Cross your right leg over your left so that your left foot is behind your right knee, trapping your opponent's arm and head between your legs. Squeeze with your legs by pulling your legs towards yourself in order to apply the strangulation technique. This technique can be done in many other situations, but only if you have a hold on both the head and the arm, as applying the stranglehold to the head only is not permitted.

⇨ **Tsukkomi jime (Thrusting strangle)**

This technique is executed when you are above your opponent. Your left hand takes hold of her lapel on the same side and pulls down to tighten the collar.

With your right hand, take hold of the other lapel with your thumb pointing downwards and push it across her throat (right) and down her shoulder, using your body weight to apply the strangulation technique.

Stopping strangles

There are several different ways to stop or escape from strangles; below are examples of a few of the most common methods.

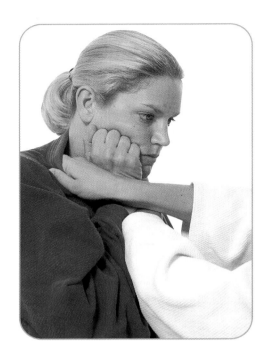

⇨   Placing your hand between the strangling edge — in this case, your opponent's arm — and your neck is very effective if done correctly. It is very important that you make a fist, which you place against your cheek; if your hand is open, your wrist can bend under your chin and you may well end up being strangled by your own arm.

⇧   Turning your head away from the strangulation — usually into your opponent's armpit — is yet another way of escaping the strangulation hold of an opponent. This will give you a short respite and should always be used in conjunction with another method of escape.

⇧   Tucking your head in is another way of avoiding strangulation. This is done by raising both shoulders and placing your chin firmly against your chest so that nothing can be placed against your throat; your hands are used to protect the sides of your neck.

Mastering arm locks

In competition judo, all arm locks are executed against the elbow joint. These arm locks can be applied by using various parts of the body as a fulcrum. There are two types of arm locks:

- bent-arm locks where the elbow joint is bent, and
- straight-arm locks where the arm is straight.

The following examples are some of the more commonly used techniques, all of which can be performed from different positions.

⇨ **Ude gatame (Arm lock)**

As your opponent pushes you upwards while turning towards you, stop his body from turning and control him by placing your knee just above his hip. Lock his hand to your shoulder, using your head to trap it there. Place both hands just below his elbow joint with your thumbs above and apply pressure towards your own body to apply the arm lock. This technique is usually executed as your opponent attempts to escape from a holding technique.

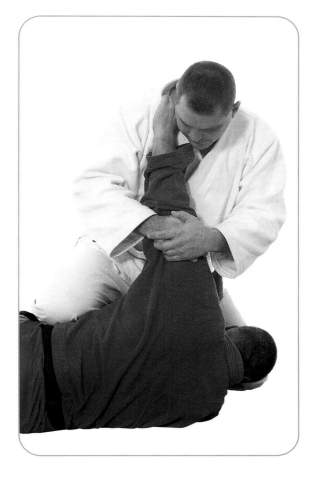

⇦ **Juji gatame (Cross lock)**

This can be done on either arm. Your opponent is on his back, while your legs are across his body, with his upper arm clamped between your thighs. Control his arm and body with your legs. With both hands, hold his arm at his wrist so he is unable to rotate his hand and his thumb points up. Pull down on his arm while raising your hips to apply the lock. This technique can be done in many ways — including upside down with one leg across the body — after a throw or as a turnover.

⇦ **Ude garami (Entangled arm lock) (1)**

Your opponent is on his back and you are lying across his chest, holding the opposite arm, as he tries to push you away. With the hand nearest his head, take hold of his hand at the wrist and push it down so that his hand points towards his head. Slide your other hand under his arm and take hold of your own wrist so that your forearm is in the crook of his elbow. Lift your arm slightly to raise his elbow; then pull his hand towards you to apply the lock. If done properly, this lock works on the elbow and not the shoulder. This arm lock can be done on either side.

⇦ **Ude garami (Entangled arm lock) (2)**

This lock is similar to the *ude garami* (above), except that your opponent's hand points down. As he tries to push you away, use your hand nearest his feet to take hold of his wrist and push it down so that his hand points to his feet. Slide your other hand under his arm and hold your own wrist so your forearm is in the crook of his elbow. Lift slightly with your arm to raise his elbow; pull his hand towards you to apply the lock. This lock works on the elbow and not the shoulder, and can be done on either side.

⇦ **Ude garami (Entangled arm lock) (3)**

Your opponent is between your legs. Pull your opponent down so that his chest is against your stomach and push his head to the right. With your left hand, reach over his right shoulder and take hold of his right wrist with your thumb at the bottom. Push your right hand through the gap between his arm and body, and take hold of your own wrist with your thumb pointing downwards so that your forearm is in the crook of his elbow. Pull up towards his head with your right hand to apply the lock.

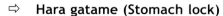

⇨ **Hara gatame (Stomach lock)**

You are holding your opponent on his right side in *kuzure kesa gatame*. He manages to free himself and turns away from you. As he turns, keep control of his right arm and move around the top of his head. Pull his arm across your body and place his elbow just below your stomach, with his thumb pointing away from you. Pull back on his wrist and push your hips forward to apply the arm lock.

⇨ **Waki gatame (Armpit lock) (1)**

You are holding your opponent on his left side in *kesa gatame*. He manages to free himself and turns away from you. As he turns, again keep control of his left arm and move around the top of his head, until you are on the other side and are able to place your left elbow over his left arm, trapping his upper arm in your armpit. With both hands, control his wrist and arm, thereby ensuring that his thumb is facing the floor. Lift up with both hands — while bearing down with your armpit — to apply the armpit lock. This technique can be done as effectively on the opposite side.

⇨ **Waki gatame (Armpit lock) (2)**

You are in a standing position, and your opponent is facing you. As he reaches towards you with his left hand, take hold of and control his hand and wrist so that his thumb is pointing towards the floor. Pull him forward off balance and turn to your left. Step in front of his feet with your right foot and put your right arm over his arm. Continue to pull on his arm until you are able to trap his upper arm under your armpit. Lift up with both hands while bearing down with your armpit to apply the armpit lock. This technique can also be done on the opposite side.

⇧ **Preventing arm locks**

Your opponent is attempting to apply a *juji gatame*. As he steps across your head and sits down to apply the lock, throw your feet up over your head and roll over your shoulder — the one nearest to him — and onto your knees. This action rotates your body and arm out of the lock and places you above your opponent in an attacking position. Of course, if his leg prevents you from rolling, you will have to attempt an alternative — and, often, a more advanced — manoeuvre.

STANDING & THROWING

Throwing techniques are the most visually exciting part of competition judo, irrespective of the stature of the *judoka*. Competitors combine timing, speed and skill with control to execute some of the most decisive techniques in judo and, when done correctly, these manoeuvres seem almost effortless.

Kuzushi — breaking balance

Successful throwing techniques in judo are based on *kuzushi* — the breaking or control of your opponent's balance (see page 61). It is, however, difficult to break that balance unless you start from a position in which you have control over your own balance.

There are six basic postures, which you should understand before attempting to break balance.

■ **Natural posture:** you stand in a relaxed, upright position with your feet shoulder-width apart, but not wider.

■ **Right natural posture:** the same position as above, but with the right foot forward.

■ **Left natural posture:** the same position as above, but with the left foot forward.

■ **Defensive posture:** Again, the body should be upright, but with the feet wider than shoulder-width apart and the knees slightly bent.

■ **Right defensive posture:** the same position as above, but with the right leg forward.

■ **Left defensive posture:** the same position as above, but with the left leg forward.

In the illustrations on page 61, the breaking of balance is demonstrated standing still. This is even more effective if applied while your opponent is moving. Although power may seem the most important factor in competitive judo, especially among heavyweight *judoka*, this power can only be utilized effectively against an opponent of equal strength if the basic principles of *kuzushi* are correctly applied.

Kumikata — taking hold

The practice of *kumikata* (taking hold of your opponent, either on his or her body or their *gi* in order to execute a follow-up manoeuvre) is one of the fundamental aspects of judo. *Kumikata* (see page 60) is vital to the success of a move because, without being able to hold correctly, it is very difficult to execute *kuzushi* (breaking of balance) and to control your movement. It is very important that you practise your attacking techniques from as many different holding positions as possible as you may only have one chance of getting a hold and maintaining control.

Tai sabaki

Tai sabaki (or body shifting and body control) is the use of your body to prevent a throw, and can be divided into two categories: the first being avoiding throws and attacks and the second, blocking throws and attacks.

Avoiding an attack

In trying to avoid a throw, it is important to prevent your opponent making body contact as this will allow you space in which to move. It is also important to maintain the correct posture so that you are able to move quickly and efficiently (see page 73).

Blocking an attack

In blocking throws, you should break your opponent's control of your arms, and use your hips to block the opponent's movements by bending your knees as you rotate your hips. In so doing, you also stabilize your own balance and posture.

opposite IN THE 2000 OLYMPIC FINALS, INOUE KOSEI OF JAPAN TAKES GOLD WITH IPPON FOR *UCHI MATA* FROM SILVER MEDALLIST NICOLAS GILL OF CANADA.

Kumikata — taking hold

⇧ Face your opponent (blue) in a natural posture with feet slightly apart. Reach forward with your right hand and take hold of her collar, with your thumb at the top. Take her right sleeve — near the elbow underneath the arm — with your hand cupped and thumb to the outside.

⇧ Control the right sleeve of your opponent with your left hand, holding her collar with your right hand. Then, with your right hand under her armpit, take hold of her belt at the back. While you are doing this, step forward with your right foot so that you are able to maintain your own balance.

⇧ In some of the throws in judo, it may be necessary to control both your opponent's sleeves.

⇧ Maintaining control by holding both lapels may be used in *sutemi waza* (sacrifice) techniques.

Kuzushi — breaking balance

⇐ The opponent's balance is broken forward. With both you and your opponent standing in the natural posture, hold her collar with your right hand, and her sleeve with the left. Step back sharply with your left foot, pulling forward and up with both hands. Keep your right elbow down and close to your opponent's chest while pulling her up and forward onto her toes.

⇐ Your opponent's balance is broken backward. In the natural posture, hold her left collar with your right hand and her right sleeve with your left. Pull with both hands, placing your right foot between her feet. Push her right elbow in to her body, keeping your elbow close to her chest.

⇐ Your opponent's balance is being broken to her right. Start in the natural posture and step sharply to your left, while pulling out and up on your opponent's right elbow. Your right hand should also pull her across your body to your left.

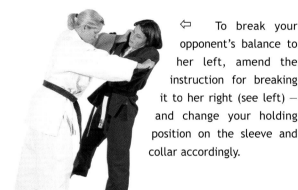

⇐ To break your opponent's balance to her left, amend the instruction for breaking it to her right (see left) — and change your holding position on the sleeve and collar accordingly.

⇐ Break your opponent's balance towards her right front. From the natural posture, step back with your left foot, forcing her to step forward with her right foot. Continue to pull and prop her onto the outside front edge of her right foot. Keep your right elbow close to her chest while pulling up and out with your left hand.

⇐ From the right holding posture, break your opponent's balance towards her left. From the natural posture, pull slightly forward. As she pulls back, step forward with your right foot. Pull down with your right hand, pushing her weight onto the outside edge of her left foot, rocking her onto the back of her left heel. Practise these methods to the left and right, from a stationary and then moving stance.

⇩ Uki-goshi (Floating hip throw)

One of the original techniques of judo, this is a very effective self-defence technique. Otherwise known as the Floating hip throw, *uki-goshi* uses a springing action of the body, combined with the hip action of *o-goshi*. The legs, however, are not bent but snapped towards your opponent to give lift for the throw. Take hold of your opponent's right sleeve with your left hand and break his balance forward to his right front corner. Place your right arm under his left arm, with your hand between his shoulder blades.

⇧ Place your right foot between his feet, close to his right foot.

⇧ Snap your left foot in to your right foot; lift him onto your hips.

⇧ Rotate your hips and throw him forward and over your body.

⇩ Ogoshi (Large hip throw)

Many of the throwing techniques in judo are derived from the hip throw. This basic technique teaches the use of the hips and legs to throw. It is very important to use the legs and not just the back to lift.

The strength that is utilized in the execution of this throw comes from a combination of hips, legs and back, with the arms locking your opponent onto your back and hips.

⇦ You have to rotate your body in front of your opponent. Your left hand controls your opponent's right sleeve and your right hand is placed behind his back, holding his belt.

⇦ Now pull your opponent up onto your hips while bending your knees, and lift him with your legs and arms, rolling him over your hips.

⇨ **Morote seoi nage
(Two-handed shoulder throw)**

Face your opponent in the right natural posture. With your left hand, pull on her right sleeve, turning your hand clockwise so your little finger is on top as you pull. Step forward and across with your right foot. Keep hold of her left lapel with your right hand and slip your elbow across her chest so it is tucked in under her armpit, turning your body so that her chest is against your shoulder blades. Continue turning; bring your left foot in line with your right. Knees should be bent, with your opponent locked against your back (right). Your body must be upright. The left hand maintains the pull.

↗ In the follow-through, throw your opponent forward over your shoulder.

⇦ **Ippon seoi nage
(One-arm shoulder throw)**

Face your opponent and take hold in the right natural posture. With your left hand, pull on his right sleeve, and turn your hand clockwise so your little finger is on top as you pull.

Then step forward and across with your right foot, while placing your right arm under his armpit so that you trap his upper arm in the crook of your arm, turning your body so that his chest is against your shoulder blades. Your left hand maintains the pulling action throughout the movement.

↗ Continue turning, bringing your left foot in line with your right foot. Both knees should be slightly bent, with your opponent locked against your back. Straighten your legs as you lean forward to lift him.

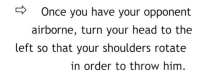

⇨ Once you have your opponent airborne, turn your head to the left so that your shoulders rotate in order to throw him.

⇦ **Eri seoi nage (Lapel shoulder throw)**

Stand facing your opponent, holding her in the right natural posture. With your left hand, pull on her right sleeve, turning your hand clockwise so that your little finger is on top as you pull. Step forward and across with your right foot. With your right hand, let go of her left lapel and take hold of her right lapel. Slip your elbow across her chest so that it is tucked in under her armpit, turning your body so that your opponent's chest is against your shoulder blades (left). Continue turning your body, bringing your left foot back in line with your right foot.

⇦ Both knees should be slightly bent, with your opponent locked against your back; your torso must be straight. The left hand maintains the pulling action throughout the movement. Continue to bend your knees and lift your opponent onto your back.

⇨ Now straighten your legs as you lean forward to lift your opponent. Once you have your opponent airborne, turn your head to the left so that your shoulders are able to rotate as you throw her.

Osoto gari (Large outer reap)

⇩   Take hold in the right natural posture; step forward with your left foot and place it outside of your opponent's right leg. As you step, push forward with your left hand and lift with your right so his body is tipped to his right rear.

⇦   Transfer your weight to your left leg as you bring your right leg forward and up behind his left leg.

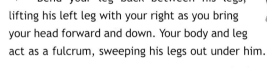

⇨   Bend your leg back between his legs, lifting his left leg with your right as you bring your head forward and down. Your body and leg act as a fulcrum, sweeping his legs out under him.

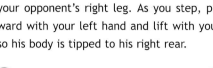

⇦   ## Ouchi gari (Large inner reap)

Take hold in the right natural posture; step forward between your opponent's legs with your right leg. Push his left shoulder backwards with your right hand, while pulling slightly with your left hand on his right sleeve, breaking his balance to the left rear corner.

⇨   Bring your right leg back, hooking his left leg and pulling it forward to throw. Try not to lift your foot entirely off the ground as you pull it back.

⬈   Bring your left leg to your right leg and transfer your weight to it. Lift his left leg from the inside with your right, unbalancing him.

Tai otoshi (Body drop)

This popular technique is used in an attack and counter attack.

⇩ Place your right foot midway between your opponent's feet to break his balance to his front right.

⇩ Control his right sleeve with your left hand. Your right hand holds his left lapel; keep your right elbow down, close to his chest. Bring your left foot in towards your right. Snap your right leg across, in front of his right leg below his knee.

⇩ Continue the hand action and the rotation of your body and throw your opponent forward over your right leg.

Koshi guruma (Hip wheel)

This technique can be used against an opponent who is fighting with the body bent forward from the waist.

⇧ Place your right arm over her shoulder; pull her right arm across your chest and break her balance. Place your right foot in front of hers.

⇧ Step your left foot in towards your right. Rotate your hips in front of her, throwing your weight forward while continuing the rotation.

⇧ Now complete the throw by rolling your opponent forward over your hips.

Kouchi gari (Small inner reap)

⇧ As your opponent steps forward with his right leg, step between his legs with your right leg. Pull on his left arm with your right hand and push his right shoulder back to break his balance with his weight on his right foot.

⇧ Place your left foot next to your right, and transfer your weight to your left leg. Turn your right foot and place the sole behind his right ankle. Using your foot, hook his right foot forward in the direction of his toes.

⇧ Continue pulling his foot forward until he is no longer able to maintain his balance and he is thrown to the floor.

Kosoto gari (Small outer reap)

⇧ As your opponent steps forward on his right leg, step forward outside that leg with your left. Push his right elbow across to your right with your left hand as you lift and push over his left shoulder with your right.

⇧ With your left heel, hook his right leg on the outside.

⇧ Continue to hook and draw his foot forwards until he falls.

Uchimata
(Inner thigh reaping throw)

⇦ Take hold in the right natural posture with your right hand high up on your opponent's left lapel. Step forward with your right foot and place it between his feet with your toes pointing to your left. Pivoting to the left on the ball of your right foot, place your left foot outside your partner's left foot while pulling on his right arm with your left hand and pushing on his left collar so that you twist his shoulders.

⇦ Continue pulling and pushing with your hands. Transfer your weight to your left leg and sweep back with your right leg.

⇧ Continue lifting your right leg and drop your head to your knee as you lift your opponent's left leg into the air.

⇧ The throwing action is continued until your opponent is successfully thrown to the ground.

Harai goshi (Hip sweep)

➡ Take hold in the right natural posture, with your right hand high up on your opponent's left lapel. Step forward with your right foot and place it between his feet with your toes pointing to your left. Bring your left foot back to your right so that your toes point away from your partner as you pull with your left hand and push with your right to force his weight onto his right foot.

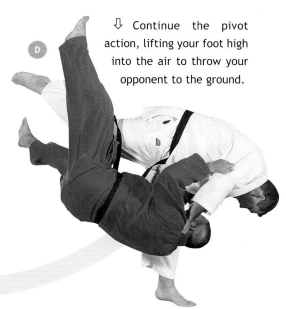

⬅ Bring your right leg forward and pull your opponent forward and up against your hip and back.

⬇ Continue the pivot action, lifting your foot high into the air to throw your opponent to the ground.

⬅ Keep your opponent tight against your body and sweep your right leg back, sweeping your opponent's legs off the floor by pivoting around on your left leg.

Okuriashi harai (Foot sweep)

⇧ As your opponent moves towards his left side, sweep his right foot towards his left foot with the sole of your left foot. Break his balance by lifting him.

⇧ Using both hands, continue the lift and then sweep, while rotating the opponent's shoulders.

⇩ This action will turn your opponent as he is lifted off the mat, throwing him onto his back.

Deashi harai (Forward foot sweep)

⇧ Hold in the right natural posture. When your opponent steps forward with his right foot, pull him forward and across to his right. At the same time, sweep his right foot with the sole of your left foot.

⇧ Continue to rotate your opponent's shoulder towards his right, while at the same time sweeping his right foot up and off the ground with the sole of your left foot.

⇧ Twist your opponent's body with both your hands, throwing him down onto his back — but it is important to sweep up his right advancing foot before it makes contact with the mat.

Tani otoshi (Valley drop)

This can be used as an attack or counterattack.

⇐ With your right hand, hold the left collar of your opponent. When she steps back with her right leg and tries to prevent you taking hold with your left hand, grab her left leg with your left hand.

⇐ Keep a tight hold on her leg and place your right leg as far as possible across behind her legs.

⇩ Roll backwards onto your right side, while throwing your opponent backwards over your outstretched right leg.

⇨ Pull down to the back with your right hand on her collar, while lifting her left leg.

Morote gari (Two-handed reap)

This powerful throw is very popular in Eastern Europe, largely because of the region's long history of wrestling.

✍ As your opponent tries to take hold, step forward with your right leg and grab the back of her legs with both hands. Place your right shoulder by the knot of her belt, making sure that your head is next to her right hip on the outside.

⇨ Push with your shoulder while you lift your opponent's legs, throwing her onto her back. It is very important that this is done in one smooth movement, or your opponent can twist out of the throw because you will have no control over the top of her body.

Tomoe nage (Circular throw)

This is a very popular throw in competitive judo, and there are many variations of the basic technique.

⇧ Your opponent pushes you. Push back with your right leg forward and move your left hand from his right sleeve to his right collar. Lift with both hands, breaking his balance forward.

⇧ Step forward with your left foot, sliding your left leg between his legs, and roll onto your back, placing the sole of your right foot in front of his left hip.

⇧ Continue to pull with both hands, pushing up with your right leg and throwing your opponent over your left shoulder.

Ura nage (Back throw)

This powerful throw, used mainly as a counterattack, is a popular throw in judo, particularly in Europe.

⇩ Block by bending your knees. Grab your opponent's belt with your left hand, placing your right hand in front of his stomach.

↰ Continue the lift and the rotation, throwing him over your left shoulder as you fall onto your left back shoulder.

↗ Use your legs, arms and back muscles to lift him, and rotate left.

Tai sabaki

Avoiding throws

⇨ The defender (right) has stopped the body contact by using her left hand, and has started to jump around the throw.

↗ The defender moves part of the way around the attack in order to prevent herself being thrown.

⇧ In the jump, your feet are wide apart to allow you to land in a stable position. You can also avoid the throw by moving in the opposite direction to the attack.

↗ The attacker has dropped onto her knees to throw. Prevent contact by moving back and to your opponent's left, using the momentum to jump around the throw.

↗ When landing, try to do so on both feet to allow you to turn your opponent onto her back. You will now be in a position to attack with a groundwork technique.

Blocking throws

⇦ If your opponent (right) attacks with a right-sided throw, block by pulling your right arm loose and push your left hip forward, while stepping back with your right leg. At the same time, bend your left knee. This will break your opponent's body contact and stabilize your balance.

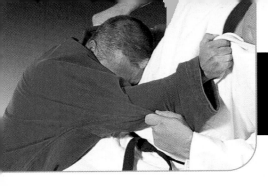

ADVANCED TECHNIQUES

dvanced techniques in judo are essentially basic throwing manoeuvres that have been specifically adapted or changed in order to throw an experienced opponent or partner. Some throws may be done on the 'incorrect' side or from an unorthodox holding position. A sequence of throws may also be linked together, or executed in succession, to form combinations of two or more throws. Judo is constantly changing because of these variations, and new ways of executing throws are always being developed.

Combinations

Experienced *judoka* can see and stop a judo throw due to the training and practice of the techniques used. By attacking with one throw, which the opponent blocks, then doing a different throw using his escaping action, you can throw an experienced opponent. Combinations can be done in various ways (left—left, left—right, forward—backward and vice versa). Multiple techniques can also be linked; one may use many throws in a sequence in order to throw an opponent.

above TECHNICALLY ADVANCED MOVEMENTS MAY ALLOW A COMPETITOR TO OVERPOWER EVEN THE MOST SKILLED OPPONENT.

opposite MANY OF THE ADVANCED THROWING TECHNIQUES REQUIRE BOTH SKILL AND SPLIT-SECOND PRECISION.

Osoto gari to harai goshi (Large outer reap to sweeping hip throw)

⇧ Your opponent (left) blocks the *osoto gari*, pushing you back.

⇧ Change your hand action from pushing to pulling as you pivot right on your left leg by hopping on the spot. You will then face the same direction as your opponent.

⇧ Sweep your leg back and throw with *harai goshi* (sweeping hip throw).

Kouchi gari to ippon seoi nage (Small inner reap to one-arm shoulder throw)

⇧ After attacking with *kouchi gari*, your opponent (left) lifts her foot out of the way and steps back.

⇧ Pull on her right sleeve with your left hand to break her balance to the front. Pivot on the right foot and bring the left in line with the right, knees bent, as you slip your right arm under her right arm.

⇧ From the position in which your knees are bent to hold the weight of your opponent, straighten your legs, and then turn your head to the left to throw your opponent with a one-arm shoulder throw.

Koshi guruma to tani otoshi
(Hip wheel to valley drop)

⇐ In this throwing sequence, you use a forward-throwing action so that you are able to use your opponent's resistance to throw her to the rear.

⇐ As your opponent bends her knees to resist the attack and pulls back, maintain your hold on her sleeve and jacket, shifting your weight to your left leg and bringing your right leg back and behind her.

⇨ Place your leg as far as possible across and behind your opponent's legs. Pull down on the jacket at the back of her neck with your right hand. Bend your left knee and roll your body to the right, throwing your opponent over your outstretched right leg.

It is important that you turn your body as much as possible so that you land on your right side and not on your back. This will put you in a good position to follow up with a groundwork attack if you are unable to score maximum points for the throw.

Kouchi gari to uchimata
(Small inner reap to inner thigh reaping throw)

⇨ Your opponent will be able to avoid the right-handed attack of *kouchi gari* if he lifts his right foot out of the way and takes a step backwards with that foot.

⇦ Pull on your opponent's left sleeve with your right hand and push his head towards his right to break his balance and rotate his shoulders. At the same time, pivot on your right foot, bringing your left foot back past the outside of his left leg.

⇩ Continue to pull on your opponent's right sleeve and transfer your body weight to your left leg.

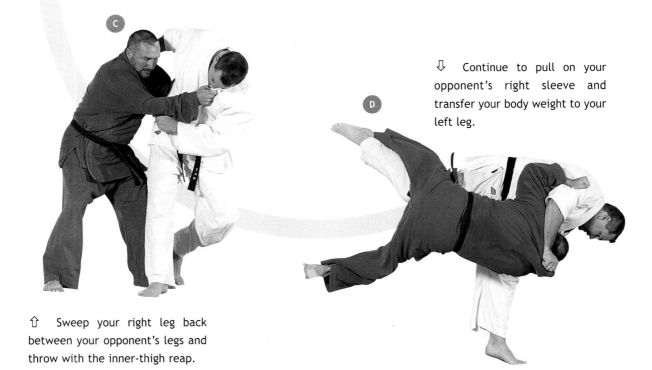

⇧ Sweep your right leg back between your opponent's legs and throw with the inner-thigh reap.

Counter throws

Counter throws are used to throw an opponent using her entry or exit from an attack. Some require blocking and stopping the movement while others rely on avoiding the movement.

Tai otoshi counter kosoto gake (Body drop counter small outer hook)

↘ Your partner attacks with a body drop or *tai otoshi*.

⇦ To avoid the attack, step over your opponent's right leg with your right leg. Place your right foot slightly in front of her feet, turning towards her.

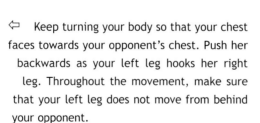

⇦ Keep turning your body so that your chest faces towards your opponent's chest. Push her backwards as your left leg hooks her right leg. Throughout the movement, make sure that your left leg does not move from behind your opponent.

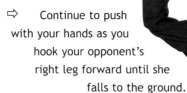

⇨ Continue to push with your hands as you hook your opponent's right leg forward until she falls to the ground.

Uchimata counter tai otoshi
(Inner thigh reaping throw counter body drop)

⇐ Your opponent attacks you with left-handed *uchimata*.

↗ To avoid your opponent's technique, move your leg out of the way and to the side as his leg sweeps back to catch yours. At the same time, pull his right arm towards you with your left hand and push his left shoulder away using your right hand.

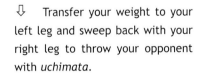

⇒ Slip your right leg across in front of your opponent's legs and throw him by pulling him around your leg.

Kosoto gari
counter uchimata
(Small outer reap counter
inner thigh reaping throw)

⇧ Block your opponent's *kosoto gari* attack by ensuring that your stance is rigid so that your body is not tipped backwards. Pull your opponent's right sleeve to break his balance to his right front corner.

⇧ Pivoting on your right leg, move your left leg back to place it outside your opponent's left leg.

⇩ Transfer your weight to your left leg and sweep back with your right leg to throw your opponent with *uchimata*.

Counter to foot sweeps
Deashi harai to tsubame gaeshi
(Forward foot sweep to swallow counter)

This is a very useful counter attack against an opponent who has attempted to sweep without first breaking your balance.

⇨ Your opponent tries to sweep your left foot with her right foot without breaking your balance.

⇦ Pull your left foot back, while maintaining control of your opponent's right sleeve and left collar (left). As her right leg passes your retracted left foot, turn her shoulders with your hands, quickly bringing your left foot forward.

⇨ As you bring your left foot forward, sweep her right foot with the sole of your left foot, continue the sweeping action initiated by your opponent to throw your her onto her back.

Throws to holds
Osoto gari to kesa gatame

The *osoto gari* (large outer reap) to *kesa gatame* (scarf hold) is a powerful combination because the follow-through to the hold helps to ensure full body commitment to the throw.

⇨ As your opponent steps forward with her right leg, break her balance to her right back corner and step forward with your left foot, swinging your right leg forward and up.

⇨ Using the back of your right leg, reap the back of your opponent's right thigh. Rotate her left shoulder to the mat, while pulling her right arm in towards your chest.

↯ Follow your opponent down to the mat, while maintaining control of her right arm. As she hits the mat, slide your right arm around her neck and lock her right arm under your left armpit. Place your head down, close to her head, with your feet wide apart, your right leg forward and your left leg back.

Ippon seoi nage counter sukui nage
(One-armed shoulder throw counter scooping throw)

⇦ As your partner attacks with the right *ippon seoi nage*, you counter by moving around his body to his right so that your opponent's back cannot make contact with your chest.

⇨ Once you get to his right side, your feet should be spread apart to provide good balance. Bend your knees, keep hold of his collar with your right hand and, using your left hand, reach between his legs from behind and gathering his leg to you to clamp his right thigh to your chest.

⇦ Lift your left hand up and pull your right hand down to roll your opponent onto his back.

⇧ Keeping your opponent clamped close to your body, straighten your legs and lift your opponent to your chest.

Ippon seoi nage to yoko shiho gatame
(One-armed shoulder throw to side-locking four-corner hold)

This throw is a modification of the basic *ippon seoi nage* and, besides being difficult to block using the hips, is also very useful against an opponent who fights with stiff arms because you can attack by slipping in under your opponent's arms.

⇐ Take tight control of your opponent's right arm, and break her balance forward and up. Raise your upper right arm under her right arm, locking hers in the bend of your right elbow. Spin in and drop on both knees between your opponent's legs.

⇨ Pull down hard on your opponent's right arm while rotating your shoulders to the left. Make sure that you turn your head to look over your left shoulder, and then throw your opponent forward and over your shoulders.

⇨ Follow up the throw with *yoko shiho gatame* by placing your right arm between her legs and grabbing her belt or jacket. Place your left arm under her head and, with your left hand, take hold of the left side of her collar. Make sure that you have tight control of your opponent's chest.

Tai otoshi to juji gatame
(Body drop to cross lock)

⬅ Throw your partner with right *tai otoshi*.

↘ As she falls to the ground, pull up on her right arm and step across her head with your left foot. Sit down as close as possible against her left shoulder.

⬇ Keeping control of the arm, lay back as you bring your right leg across her chest. Clamp your knees together, apply the arm lock by pulling down on her hand so her thumb points away from you.

Tomoe nage to tate shiho gatame
(Circular throw to four-corner hold)

⬆ Throw your your opponent with *tomoe nage*, using both feet and keeping close contact with his body.

⬆ Staying in contact, throw your feet over your shoulder so that when your opponent lands on his back, you land astride him and are able hold him in *tate shiho gatame*.

Competitive judo

The referee's signals and instructions in competitive judo are important elements of competition.

Aizu — principal signals

A *Ippon* (one point; complete point): raise arm above the head with palm forward.

B *Waza-ari* (technique exists): raise one arm sideways at shoulder height, with the palm down.

C *Waza-ari-awasete-ippon*: *waza-ari*, then *ippon* gesture.

D *Yuko* (effective): raise one arm with palm down, 45° from the body.

E *Koka* (minor score): raise the bent arm with the thumb towards the shoulder, and the elbow kept close to the body.

F *Osaekomi* (hold is on): facing and bending towards the contestants, stretch out your arms towards them.

G *Osaekomi-toketa* (hold broken): bending your body towards the contestants, raise one arm to the front and then wave it from right to left quickly two or three times.

H *Matte!* (Wait!): raise one hand to shoulder height, with the arm parallel to the *tatami*, and display the flat palm of the hand.

I *Hantei* (judgement): in preparation of calling *hantei*, raise the hands at 45° with the correct flag in each hand; at the announcement of *hantei*, raise the flags high.

J *Sono mama* (hold positions): indicated verbally and by leaning foward and touching both contestants with the palms of the hand.

Aizu — additional signals

■ Instruction to adjust the *judo gi*: cross left hand over right, palms facing inwards, at belt height.

■ Recording a medical examination: hand opened towards contestant; with the other, raise index finger towards the recorder for first examination and the index and middle-finger for the second.

■ Penalty (*shido, chui, keikoku, hansoku-make*): point to contestant with index finger extended from a fist.

■ Non-combativity: rotate forearms forward at chest height and point with forefinger at the contestant.

■ Cancellation of an expressed opinion: repeat with one hand the scoring gesture, while raising the other above the head to the front, waving it from right to left two or three times.

See also the definitions in the Glossary on page 94.

The points system

The referee announces the points when, in his or her opinion, a technique corresponds to the following:

Ippon (10 points — maximum)

■ The contestant with control throws the other (largely on his back) with considerable force and speed.

■ A contestant holds with *osaekomi-waza* the other contestant, who is unable to get away for 25 seconds after the announcement of *osaekomi*.

■ A contestant submits (taps twice or says *maitta)*.

■ A contestant is incapacitated by a *shime-waza* or *kansetsu-waza*.

Waza-ari (7 points — near maximum)

■ The contestant with control throws the other, but the technique is lacking in one of four elements necessary for *ippon*.

■ A contestant holds with *osaekomi-waza* the other, who is unable to get away for 20—25 seconds.

Yuko (5 points)

■ A contestant with control throws the other, but the technique is lacking in two of *ippon* elements:

(1) Partially lacking in the element of 'largely on the back' and lacking in either 'speed' or 'force'.

(2) Partially lacking in both 'speed' and 'force'.

■ A contestant holds with *osaekomi-waza* the other, who is unable to get away for 15—20 seconds.

Koka (3 points)

■ A contestant with control throws the other onto one shoulder, the thigh(s) or buttocks with both speed and force.

■ A contestant holds with *osaekomi-waza* the other, who is unable to get away for 10—15 seconds.

S ELF-DEFENCE

The self-defence techniques in judo originate from jujutsu, and are usually taught in *kata* or set forms. These can be divided into the original jujutsu techniques (such as *Kime no Kata*) or the more modern forms, called *Kodokan Goshinjutsu*. The Japanese Police and Security Services, for example, practise the *kodokan-goshin-jutsu* techniques on a daily basis and they form an essential part of the security forces' training programme.

It is essential to realize that self-defence techniques can only be effective if practised regularly, as this will develop smooth and effective manoeuvres and a heightened sense of body movement and control.

We have illustrated on the following pages just some of the techniques that are learnt as part of judo self-defence. These should only be practised under the supervision of a qualified coach, in suitable surroundings — and on the appropriate surface — to avoid injury because these techniques are dangerous if executed incorrectly or without proper control.

Defending yourself

Self-defence techniques in judo are based on avoiding your opponent's attacks and breaking your opponent's balance so that you are able to utilize his strength against him. Striking techniques (*atemi waza*) are also used in judo and are aimed largely at the weaker and most vulnerable parts of the body.

When defending yourself using judo, it is important to remember to execute your movements with speed, skill and precision in order to counter the strength of the attacker. A surprise attack will often knock you to the ground, leaving you flat on your back, before you have had the opportunity to react or retaliate in your own defence. Judo, however, teaches you to respond by fighting on the ground.

Self-defence techniques can, however, only be effective with continued practice so that the movements and reactions become instinctive. Practice will also help improve your coordination and awareness of your own strengths and weaknesses. It is nevertheless important that you practise only under the close supervision of a suitably qualified coach, who is able to provide constructive guidelines on technique and other safety issues.

left CLEAR AND LOGICAL THINKING WILL ASSIST YOU TO RESPOND SWIFTLY AND EFFICIENTLY TO A SURPRISE ATTACK.
opposite BREAK YOUR OPPONENT'S BALANCE BY UTILIZING HER ATTACKING MOVEMENT.

⇧ As an attacker grabs you around the shoulders, place one hand behind his back and punch him in the groin with your other.

⇧ As he bends forward from the punch, reach across to grab his right sleeve with your left hand and step across in front of him, bending your knees and picking him up on your hips.

⇧ As you lift him up, turn slightly to throw him forward over your hips.

⇦ You may be lying on your back when an attacker sits astride you in an attempt to strangle you.

⇦ Bring your arm through between the attacker's arms and try to strike him on the chin with the heel of your hand while bridging at the same time.

⬈ As you execute the bridging action, rotate your body, throwing the attacker forward and to the side.

⇧ Complete the movement by striking the attacker in the groin or stomach with your elbow.

⇧ You are attacked from behind, with your attacker grabbing you around the neck in order to strangle you.

⇧ Twist to the side, creating enough space in which to strike your attacker in the stomach with your elbow.

⇧ Clamp his arm to your chest and stamp on his foot with your left heel. Drop to one knee, throwing him forwards.

⇧ To succeed in this defensive action, it is very important that you continue the forward rotation of the throw.

⇦ If your attacker tries to kick you from the front, move to outside of the attack and catch his heel and ankle in the palm of your left hand. As you do this, step back in line to face him, lifting his foot up and twisting it to the outside to lock his ankle and knee.

↯ Kick your attacker in the groin with your right foot.

⇩ Continue to lift his leg with both hands, breaking his balance backwards and throwing him onto his back.

MAKING CONTACT

NATIONAL JUDO ASSOCIATIONS

AUSTRALIA
- JUDO FEDERATION OF AUSTRALIA
- P.O. Box 919, Glebe NSW 2037,
- Tel: (+2) 9552 2770
- Fax: (+2) 9660 8936
- E-mail: ausjudo@ausport.gov.au
- Website: www.ausport.gov.au/judo

AUSTRIA
- OESTERREICHISCHER JUDOVERBAND
- Wassergasse 26/5, 1030 Wien
- Tel: (+1) 714 71 31 33
- Fax: (+1) 714 71 31 33
- E-mail: oejv@asn.or.at
- Website: www.asn.or.at/oejv/home.htm

BELGIUM
- BELGIAN JUDO FEDERATION
- 12 Rue General Thys B-1050, Bruxelles
- Tel: (+2) 648 76 52
- Fax: (+2) 640 34 69
- E-mail: judobel@skynet.be
- Website: www.judonet.be/eng/index.html

CANADA
- JUDO CANADA
- 226-1725 St Laurent, Ottawa,
- Tel: (+613) 738 1200
- Fax: (+613) 738 1299
- E-mail: info@judocanada.org
- Website: www.judocanada.org

DENMARK
- DANISH JUDO AND JU-JITSU UNION
- Idreattens Hus, Brondby Stadion 20, DK-2605 Brondby
- Tel: (+45) 4326 2920
- Fax: (+45) 4326 2919
- E-mail: dju@dju.dk
- Website: www.dju.dk

EGYPT
- EGYPTIAN JUDO & AIKIDO FEDERATION
- Olympic Federations Complex, Cairo Stadium's Authority, Nasr City, Cairo
- Tel: (+2) 2 63 43 67
- Fax: (+2) 2 63 85 55

FINLAND
- FINNISH JUDO ASSOCIATION
Radiokatu 20, 00093 SLU
- Tel: (+9) 3481 2316
- Fax: (+9) 148 1654
- E-mail: toimisto@judolitto.fi
- Website: www.judoliitto.fi

FRANCE
- FEDERATION OF FRENCH JUDO, JUJITSU, KENDO & DISCIPLINES ASSOCIÉES
- 43 Rue des Plantes, R-75014, Paris
- Tel: (+1) 40 52 16 16
- Fax: (+1) 40 52 16 70
- E-mail: ffjudo@wanadoo.fr
- Website: www.ffjudo.com

GERMANY
- GERMAN SPORTS FORUM
- Tel: (+69) 67 60 13
- Fax: (+69) 677 22 42
- E-mail: sportforum@aol.com
- Website: www.judobund.de

GREECE
- HELLENIC JUDO FEDERATION
- Olympic Athletic Center 37, Kifisicas Ave, 151 23, Marousi
- Tel: (+1) 685 9097/689 2056
- Fax : (+1) 685 6639

IRELAND
- IRISH JUDO ASSOCIATION
- 79 Upper Dorset Street, Dublin 1
- Tel: (+1) 830 8233
- Fax: (+1) 860 0889
- E-mail: irishjudo@clubi.ie

ISRAEL
- ISRAEL JUDO ASSOCIATION
- Tel-Aviv National Sports Center, P.O. Box 58176, Tel Aviv 69482
- Tel: (+3) 647 8025
- Fax: (+3) 647 9155

ITALY
- FEDERAZIONE ITALIANA LOTTA PESI JUDO
- Viale Tiziano 70, I-00196 Roma
- Tel: (+6) 323 6659
- Fax: (+6) 324 4355
- E-mail: fijlkamit@fijlkam.it
- Website: www.fijlkam.it

KENYA
- KENYA JUDO ASSOCIATION
- P.O. Box 57847, Nairobi
- Tel: (+2) 72 25 54 / 72 42 01
- Fax: (+2) 50 11 20 (National Sports Council)

MAURITIUS
- MAURITIUS JUDO FEDERATION
- Foondhun Building, Rose Hill, Port Louis
- Tel: (+230) 464 0066 / 208 4855
- Fax: (+230) 208 7882 / 208 3799

NAMIBIA
- NAMIBIA AMATEUR JUDO
- P.O. Box 3930, Swakopmund
- Tel: (+61) 22 9285
- Fax: (+61) 23 7872

NETHERLANDS
- JUDO BOND NEDERLAND
- Blokhoeve 5, P.O. Box 7012, NL 3438 LC Nieuwegein
- Tel: (+30) 603 81 14
- Website: www.jbn.nl

NEW ZEALAND
- NEW ZEALAND JUDO FEDERATION INC.
- P.O. Box 83-180, Edmonton Road Post Office, Henderson, Auckland
- Tel: (+9) 849 2876
- Fax: (+9) 849 2854
- E-mail: office@judo.org.nz
- Website: ourworld.compuserve. com/homepages/comvirke

NORWAY
- NORGES JUDO FORBUND
- Serviceboks 1 Ulleval Stadion, N-0840 Oslo
- Tel: (+21) 02 98 20
- Fax: (+21) 02 98 21
- E-mail: judo@nif.idrett.no
- Website: www.judo.no

PORTUGAL
- FEDERACAO PORTUGUESA DE JUDO
- Rua do Quelhas 32—44, 1200-781 Lisboa
- Tel: (+351) 213 931 630
- Fax: (+351) 213 969 296
- E-mail: secretaria@fpj.pt
- Website: www.fpj.pt

SOUTH AFRICA
- JUDO SOUTH AFRICA
- P.O. Box 25680, Boksburg 1460, Gauteng
- Tel: (+12) 3 11 38 97
- Fax: (+12) 3 11 20 10
- E-mail: jsasel1@mweb.co.za
- Website: www.sportsa.co.za/sasports/judo/home.htm

SPAIN
- ROYAL SPANISH JUDO FEDERATION
- Ferraz 16, 7 Izquierda, Madrid 28008
- Tel: (+91) 559 4876
- Fax: (+91) 547 6139
- E-mail: po.roses@fbjudo.org

SWEDEN
- SWEDISH JUDO FEDERATION
- Idrottens Hus, S-12387, Farsta
- Tel: (+8) 605 6566
- Fax: (+8) 605 6567
- E-mail: info@judo.se

SWITZERLAND
- SWISS JUDO FEDERATION
- Tel: (+31) 368 05 75
- Fax: (+31) 368 05 76
- E-mail: mailto:office@sjv.ch
- Website: www.sjv.ch

UNITED KINGDOM
- BRITISH JUDO ASSOCIATION
- 7A Rutland Street, Leicester LE1 IRB, England
- Tel: (+1162) 55 9669
- Fax: (+1162) 55 9660
- E-mail: BritJudo@aol.com
- Website: www.britishjudo.org.uk

USA
- UNITED STATES JUDO INC.
- 1 Olympic Plaza — Suite 202, Colorado Springs CO 80909
- Tel: (+719) 578 4730
- Fax: (+719) 578 4733
- E-mail: usjudoexdr@aol.com
- Website: www.usjudo.org

ZIMBABWE
- ZIMBABWE JUDO ASSOCIATION
- P.O. Box 970, Harare
- Tel: (+4) 48 6432
- Fax: (+4) 49 0085

GLOSSARY

Aizu	Referees' gestures/signals	Kuzushi	Breaking of balance
Chui	Five-point penalty/warning	Matte!	Wait!
Deashi harai	Forward foot sweep	Morote gari	Two-handed reap
Do	Way	Morote seoi nage	Two-handed shoulder throw
Eri seoi nage	Lapel shoulder throw	Nami juji jime	Normal cross-handed strangle
Gyaku juji jime	Reverse cross-strangle	Ogoshi	Large hip throw
Hadaka jime	Naked or bare strangle	Okuriashi harai	Foot sweep
Hajime!	Begin!	Okuri eri jime	Sliding collar strangle
Hansoku make	10-point penalty (disqualification)	Osaekomu	To hold down
Hantei	Judgement or decision	Osaekomi waza	Pinning or hold-down techniques
Hara gatame	Stomach lock	Osoto gari	Large outer reap
Harai goshi	Hip sweep	Ouchi gari	Large inner reap
Hikiwake	Draw or tie	Randori	Free practice or free sparring
Ippon	10 points (win)	Sankaku jime	Triangular strangle
Ippon seoi nage	One-armed shoulder throw	Shihan	Master teacher
Ju	Gentle	Shiji	Receive instruction
Judo gi	Judo suit	Shime waza	Strangling techniques
Judoka	Judo student	Sono mama!	Freeze!
Juji gatame	Cross lock	Sukui nage	Scooping throw
Kamikata	Taking hold	Tai otoshi	Body drop
Kami shiho gatame	Upper four-corner hold	Tai sabaki	Body shifting and body control
Kansetsu waza	Joint- or arm-lock techniques	Tani otoshi	Valley drop
Kata	Formal exercises	Tatami	Mat
Kata gatame	Shoulder hold	Tate shiho gatame	Straight four-corner hold
Kataha jime	Single-wing strangle	Toketa!	Hold broken!
Kata juji jime	Half cross-handed strangle	Tomoe nage	Circular throw
Keikoku	Serious warning	Tsukkomi jime	Thrusting strangle
Kesa gatame	Scarf hold	Uchimata	Inner-thigh reaping throw
Kime no Kata	Decisive Technique Forms	Ude garami	Entangled arm lock
Kimete	Final point, determining winner	Ude gatame	Straight arm lock
Kodokan Goshinjutsu	Kodokan Self-defence Forms	Ukemi	Breakfall
Koka	Three points (minor score)	Uki goshi	Floating hip throw
Koshi guruma	Hip wheel	Ura nage	Back throw
Kosoto gari	Small outer reap	Waki gatame	Armpit lock
Kouchi gari	Small inner reap	Waza ari	Seven points
Kumikata	Gripping	Yoko shiho gatame	Side-locking four-corner hold
Kuzure	Modified	Yoshi!	Continue!
Kuzure kesa gatame	Modified scarf hold	Yuko	Five points